Exploding the Western

NUMBER NINETEEN

Tarleton State University Southwestern Studies in the Humanities

William T. Pilkington, General Editor

Exploding the Western

MYTHS OF EMPIRE ON THE POSTMODERN FRONTIER

Sara L. Spurgeon

TEXAS A&M UNIVERSITY PRESS | COLLEGE STATION

First edition

The paper used in this book
meets the minimum requirements
of the American National Standard
for Permanence of Paper
for Printed Library Materials, Z39.48-1984.
Binding materials have been
chosen for durability.
∞

A portion of chapter 1 was previously published as "The Sacred Hunter and the Eucharist of the Wilderness: Mythic Reconstructions in *Blood Meridian*," in *Cormac McCarthy: New Visions*, ed. James Lilly (Albuquerque: University of New Mexico Press, 2002), pp. 75–99. Reprinted by permission.

A portion of chapter 2 was previously published as "'Pledged in Blood': Truth and Redemption in Cormac McCarthy's *All the Pretty Horses*," *Western American Literature* 34, no. 1 (1999): 24–44 and was reprinted in *Bloom's Modern Critical Views: Cormac McCarthy*, ed. Harold Bloom (New York: Chelsea House Publishers, 2002), pp. 79–94 and in *Cormac McCarthy's* All the Pretty Horses: *Bloom's Guides*, ed. Harold Bloom (New York: Chelsea House Publishers, 2003).

Spurgeon, Sara L.
Exploding the Western : myths of empire on the postmodern frontier / Sara L. Spurgeon.—1st ed.
p. cm.—(Tarleton State University southwestern studies in the humanities; no. 19)
Includes bibliographical references and index.
ISBN 1-58544-403-0 (cloth : alk. paper)—
ISBN 1-58544-422-7 (pbk.: alk. paper)
1. American literature—West (U.S.)—History and criticism. 2. American literature—Southwestern States—History and criticism. 3. American literature—20th century—History and criticism. 4. Southwestern States—Intellectual life—20th century. 5. West (U.S.)—Intellectual life—20th century. 6. Western stories—History and criticism. 7. Postmodernism (Literature)—West (U.S.) 8. Frontier and pioneer life in literature. 9. Southwestern States—In literature. 10. West (U.S.)—In literature. 11. Imperialism in literature. I. Title. II. Series.
PS271.S68 2005
810.9'3278—dc22 2004020778

Contents

Preface

I did not start out as a scholar and writer knowing I wanted to write about Western or Southwestern literature. In a way, the process of discovering that I do has been a journey that returned me full circle to my childhood.

I am from Kansas, arguably West though certainly not Southwest. I grew up in Topeka, in a fairly privileged, Anglo, middle-class household. My father was an attorney but also an amateur naturalist and Western historian. In our house, the family room was dedicated to my father's Western pioneer-era antiques. (My mother's eighteenth-century English pieces ruled the dining room.) Having grown up on a working ranch south of town, my father had a special place in his heart, and on one wall of the family room, for antique farm implements and cowboying equipment. As a child, I would stare, awestruck, at the huge wooden ox yoke, over eight feet wide, that my father told me had pulled covered wagons across the Western prairies, maybe even through what was now our backyard. When I was sure I would not be caught, I would drag a chair close to the wall, climb on top of it, and reverently stroke the saddles, bridles, and fancy spurs chased with silver that hung above my head. On the mantle over the fireplace, tragically out of my reach, was mounted an enormous set of horns from the last longhorn on my father's family ranch. While the ranch was lost, like so many others, during the dustbowl years of the 1930s, our family history was not, and my father's story about helping his father and grandfather de-horn that bull, "Killer," was one of our childhood favorites.

When he was fourteen, my father's family moved to Topeka, and Dad basically became a city boy, but most of our family's weekend trips and excursions were to my father's past. My mother grew up on a tiny North Dakota farm without indoor plumbing, and she resolutely refused nostalgia for any aspect of rural life. Nonetheless, we regularly visited Dodge City and Abilene, Prairie Grasslands National Park and the oil fields of western Kansas, where we wandered for hours, squinting myopically at the dusty ground, searching for fossils and arrowheads. My father even bought tickets for my brothers and me for the last passenger run of the old Atchison, Topeka, and Santa Fe line.

All this Western Americana was fascinating to me as a child, but later, when my brothers and I became teenagers, we also became hugely embarrassed by our family's rural roots. So when I began studying and writing about literature, I had no real interest in Western works. I soon found, however, that the issues I wanted to explore stubbornly drew me again and again to this region. I was fascinated by the power of landscape and human relations with nature—and there were Ed Abbey and John Muir, Mary Hunter Austin and Terry Tempest Williams; issues of hybridity, liminality, and post-colonialism—and there were Gloria Anzaldúa and Simon Ortíz and Rudolfo Anaya; problems of representation, history, encounters between multiple cultures and races—and there were James Fenimore Cooper and Luci Tapahonso, Leslie Marmon Silko and Cormac McCarthy.

The next logical question for me to ask was why? Why should these issues continually lead me west? Why did all these writers consider themselves, or are considered by others, to be Western writers? What makes a writer regional? And is an author who writes from the West any different from a New England regionalist or a Southern regionalist?

One conclusion I reached is that, what is for me a journey back to my origins, back to my father's tales about farming and ranching on the Kansas prairies, my maternal grandmother's stories about growing up next to the Turtle Mountain Chippewa Reservation in North Dakota, is also a journey back to the origin stories of modern America. Stories of the frontier, the meeting place between two or more cultures, be they Anglo, Indian, Hispanic, or any other of the myriad groups that have come together in the United States, have become the founding myth of this country. Even more so than the Revolutionary War or the Declaration of Independence, stories about frontiers tell us who we are.

And while multiple frontiers have existed from one end of North America to the other, they have found their metaphoric home in the West. Not in the socio-political terms of Frederick Jackson Turner, who imagined a nation of Anglos made strong by their conquest of nature and any unfortunate Indians who got in their way, but in the cultural, mythopoeic sense that allows someone born and raised in Jersey City or Seattle or Atlanta to instantly recognize the red rock formations of Monument Valley, the saguaros of southern Arizona, or the rolling horizons of the Great Plains, to be able to whistle the theme music from *The Good, the Bad, and the Ugly.* In other words, the stubborn survival and continual reimagining of myth in the face of an often contradictory history.

This is not to imply, of course, that multiple cultures and ethnicities don't exist east of the Mississippi, but the ways in which the myth of the frontier has constructed our national vision of the West brings these realities to the fore. Literature from and about the West allows us to continually reimagine how multiple cultures should coexist, how humans should interact with nature, what we should think and how we should feel about our history and our future.

The continuing emergence of powerful new voices from this region is the most recent manifestation of our on-going national attempt to come to grips with issues that have not changed significantly since the 1880s, issues indeed determined in many cases by actions taken a century or more ago. As Creek poet Joy Harjo notes, the hoofbeats of Andrew Jackson rampaging across Georgia and Mississippi slaughtering native peoples in direct violation of treaties still echo through the streets of Tulsa and Albuquerque and Tucson and across reservations around the country. The new mythic stories coming from the metaphorical home of America's frontiers, she says, force us to hear and acknowledge the power of those hoofbeats and their continued existence.

Western literature is, in fact, probably the least regional literature we have. It is, more than any other, our national literature. N. Scott Momaday remarks that he does not believe American literature was born in New England and spread westward across the continent. He has seen, he claims, one of the first examples of American literature on the walls of a canyon in Utah. Human figures, broad-shouldered and twenty feet tall, stream across the sandstone cliffs like columns of gods marching from the earth. These figures, he says, believed to be between two thousand and five thousand years old, mark the true beginning of literature in America.

This is not to say that we must accept Momaday's remark as literal. One cannot point to a single instance as the moment of genesis. But rather than Utah's Grand Gallery Canyon as a symbolic birthplace of American literature, I would suggest yet another site in the Southwest as an even more powerful metaphor for literature in America: El Morró in New Mexico. A jutting headland of rock towering over an otherwise flat plain, visible for miles in any direction with a permanent source of water at its base, El Morró has become a vertical palimpsest, to borrow Daniel Cooper Alarcón's use of the term, a surface upon which multiple stories have been written and rewritten, sometimes directly over those underneath, though never entirely erasing them.

All travelers crossing those arid New Mexican plains were forced to stop for water at El Morró, and each group inscribed the sheer walls with the story of their passing. As the earth surrounding the rock eroded and dropped over time, each new group made their mark slightly below that of previous ones. Highest up are the sun signs, lightning bolts, and animal figures of the earliest inhabitants of the Americas. Below them are entire paragraphs gouged from the soft rock by Spanish conquistadors complaining in curling, old-world script of poor shelter, bad water, elusive gold, and meager financial support from Spain. Below that are the square, plain letters of the first English-speaking adventurers, followed by American cavalry officers, settlers, surveyors, and finally, modern tourists.

The stories of each group overlap those of the others through the centuries, but the progression is not neat and clear. Indians returned to scratch over the marks left by Spaniards; English words flow between figures of mountain lions and declarations of love for sweethearts left behind in Madríd and Mexico City. This, I would argue, is the symbolic birthplace of American literature, a hard and rocky cradle for the mythic stories that have shaped a modern nation and a fitting metaphor for a new vision of American literature that forces acknowledgement of languages other than English, visions other than European, myths and stories that have met and crossed and recrossed countless times.

Three outstanding scholars have guided my work on this text. Larry Evers, Judy Nolte Temple, and Daniel Cooper Alarcón tirelessly and relentlessly challenged my assumptions and provided both gentle encouragement and constructive criticism. Their inspiration, their insights, and their varied backgrounds were essential in helping me bring together the disparate writers examined here.

Exploding the Western

Introduction

> *Depend upon it, there is mythology now as there was in the time of Homer, only we do not perceive it because we ourselves live in the very shadow of it.*
>
> CORMAC McCARTHY

The object of this study is to trace the development of various forms of the frontier myth in the works of three contemporary writers, to offer critical interpretations of its meaning, and to assess its power in shaping the life, thoughts, and politics both of the nation that produced it and the rest of the world that must live with its ubiquitous, colonizing presence. The central concern of *Exploding the Western: Myths of Empire on the Postmodern Frontier* is to interrogate how the differing versions of these mythic tales and the genres in which they appear are being revisioned in a globalized world and to examine the ways in which they challenge and accommodate increasingly fluid and dangerous racial, cultural, and international borders.

The first thing we must understand in such an exploration is that myths are not history. Myths are what we wish history had been—a compressed, simplified, sometimes outright false vision of the past but a vision intended to serve a specific purpose in the present and, just as importantly, to bequeath a specific shape to the future. Myths compel belief in the culture and cultural story they present. In an increasingly connected world, bound together for better or worse by global tourism and global terrorism, CNN and the Internet, this means American myths begin to compel belief from other nations, as well. And as always, our mythic visions of ourselves and our identity as Americans continue to direct our interactions with that world. Actual, historical facts are, therefore, less important in determining present actions than the myths we make about them. The moment that some interpretation of historical fact is transformed into a precedent for future action is when history itself begins to function as myth. Myth, then, becomes the language through which a society remembers its history and attempts to understand its future.

Since the focus of this study is the modern reimagining of the myth of the frontier in the twentieth and twenty-first centuries, I have concentrated on the novel as a cultural form particularly important in shaping attitudes, beliefs, and expectations. The novel is certainly not the only form of cultural mythogenesis, but myths, like novels, are stories, narratives of culture, history, and our collective dreams of the future. As Edward Said notes, "nations themselves are narrations."[1]

As Said also points out, one of the achievements of imperialism was to bring the world closer together. Globalization has carried many of the old forms of military and political imperialism into the twenty-first century in the guise of cultural and economic imperialism. In the past, some scholars have been reluctant to apply the label of imperialism to the United States, despite a history of military aggression in the Philippines, Cuba, Puerto Rico, Haiti, Central America, China, Viet Nam, and the Middle East. Part of the traditional American myth of the frontier holds that the frontier experience created a land of freedom-loving individuals dedicated to bringing democracy, not imperial conquest, to the rest of the world. Thus part of this myth is a narrative that must carefully ignore or disguise American imperialism abroad, as well as the reality of invasion, conquest, and colonization that made possible the European settlement of the Americas.

Empire, however, is not necessarily a military relationship as in the conquest and displacement of Native Americans but can also be one in which one nation effectively controls the political sovereignty of another. This control may be achieved through economic, social, or cultural domination or overt or covert political influence. The American occupation of Iraq notwithstanding, direct military colonialism in much of the world is gone today although not, of course, in the United States, where the descendents of European colonizers still inhabit land taken by force from conquered native peoples. But American imperialism is also exported at an ever-increasing rate through media images, attitudes, myths, and other artifacts of culture. And just as in past ages of empire, colonizer and colonized continue to battle each other through rival versions of history and myth. Said claims the modern eruption of violent separatist movements and rhetoric "far from invalidating the struggle to be free from empire . . . actually prove the validity of a fundamental liberationist energy. . . . The only way to understand this energy, however, is historically" (xxi).

I would argue that we should also look at it mythically, as the expression of national(ist) narratives through which cultures and groups view history, the future, and their present place within a disturbingly unfixed and rapidly shifting world order. My method here is to focus on individual works and to read them as part of the relationship between culture and history, prophecy and myth. Of course, some books, authors, and ideas are going to be left out. I have tried to find fairly representative authors who speak from multiple sides of the experience of conquest and colonialism in the United States. My argument is that in an increasingly small and hybridized world, the new shapes of the myths generated to guide us into our history and our future are emerging from the same sites that produced the myths of the past—those places where imperialism and resistance meet, where globalization and colonialism clash and merge with history and memory.

Just as with earlier versions, the modern frontier myths produced in the texts examined here are mixed and hybridized, the often-troubled offspring of parents from multiple cultures and races coexisting in an uneasy intimacy. Contrary to some scholars' assumptions, modern American culture is neither lacking in myths nor unmarked by centuries of conquest and coexistence with native cultures and their myths. As many scholars have documented, the myths of both the European and native worlds collided and combined on the various frontiers of the Americas, and the presence of Indians and Indian myths (as well as Mexicans and other groups) have deeply impacted the shape of those myths that justify and direct American culture today.[2] The still-unresolved conflicts and tensions inherent in the history of conquest and colonization in the Americas keep traditional myths alive and demand their metamorphosis in response to the realities of life in an increasingly globalized world. At the start of the new millennium the very questions these earlier myths struggled to answer issues of national and racial identity, human interactions with the natural world, and relationships between the conqueror and the conquered—remain painfully current.[3]

For the purposes of this work, I propose the following definition of myth. Myths are narratives that are often sacred or religious in nature, although they may appear in the guise of secular stories. Although generally prose, I agree with G. S. Kirk's argument that myths can be poetic in form as well, as in the case of the *Iliad* or the Thought Woman stories in Leslie Marmon Silko's *Ceremony.* Myths are not relegated only to the dim and distant past, nor are they static or generated solely by "primitive" societies.[4] Change, as Th. P. Van Barren maintains, is a defining character of myth. Because of their sacred nature and the social importance of their functions as symbolic blueprints of actions and attitudes, norms of behavior, and societal structures, myths must be altered as a culture grows.

Before I proceed further with a discussion of myth, however, I must first define such terms as "frontier," "borderlands," "the West," and "the Southwest." I use the term "frontier" in the way Annette Kolodny has defined it—as the meeting place between two or more cultures encountering each other for the first time, often in a landscape perceived as dangerous and unfamiliar to at least one of the cultures involved. This suggests a mobility and mutability in frontiers. "Borderlands," on the other hand, are more permanent places, third countries as Gloria Anzaldúa terms them, at once separating and joining two or more cultures or nations, though like frontiers, they are often perceived as dangerous and strange by one or both sides or by those who inhabit the third country they embody. Thus there have been multiple, shifting frontiers historically crisscrossing the Americas, while the Southwestern borderlands separating and joining the United States and Mexico have been more or less stable and fixed since the twentieth century, at least geographically.

"The West" and to a lesser extent "the Southwest" are even more complex, in large part because the West especially has come to hold both a geographical and a mythological meaning in modern American culture. Numerous writers have offered definitions of the geographic West. It is often held to be that area of land west of the Mississippi River, and this seems like a perfectly acceptable definition, although it does not really address what was seen as "the West" in previous centuries, when, from the perspective of Anglo New England for instance, Daniel Boone was traversing "the West" in the wilds of Kentucky. Historically in North America, frontiers often, though not always, moved west and in the modern American imagination that geographic term has come to be conflated with the idea, indeed the myth, of frontiers.

The Southwest can be seen as a condensation of the West, containing all the mythic elements commonly associated with both the West and frontiers while concentrating them in the vicinity of the borderlands between the United States and Mexico. This region is seen as intensifying the idea of a harsh and difficult landscape and a feeling of exciting but ominous closeness between multiple races and cultures. Both the myth of the frontier and of the West are shot through with the twinned tropes of the perceived danger and rewards of conquering a wild, hostile landscape, and the perceived danger and rewards of conquering a wild, hostile racial Other. The Southwest, with its arid deserts and mountains, its numerous native tribes and peoples, as well as the largest population of Spanish speakers outside of Mexico, handily accommodates both strains.

But what exactly is the myth of the frontier? Beverly Stoeltje argues that the concept of frontier as used in reference to the Anglo American historical experience must be analyzed not simply as a powerful metaphor, but as a myth, specifically a version of "the bringing of civilization" (239). This myth provides the illusion that "the right forces are in control, that 'we' are winning in a battle against 'them'" (240). In America, this variant of a minor myth has become one of the most powerful shapers of national identity. One reason for this privileging of the frontier myth and its racialization is the circumstance of the European colonization of the Americas. In much of Europe the traditional hero journey in which the hero leaves his home, battles the forces of evil, and is triumphantly reborn into a new life glorifying his civilization was an individual experience; in the American colonies it became a communal one. Every early colonist experienced the terror of the long sea voyage (albeit some in more comfortable quarters than others), everyone was a stranger in the new land, everyone was equally threatened by its apparently hostile wilderness and hostile native inhabitants. These communal experiences, codified into myth, would eventually become the basis of the modern myth of the frontier.

Based on Bronislaw Malinowski's observation that myth surfaces and flourishes in times of social and historical change and that myth replicates and validates social structures, Stoeltje argues that the modern American myth of the frontier was born at the close of the nineteenth century, when interactions between competing ideological currents and everyday social life "created the conditions for the emergence of a specific national myth in the U.S. A myth more relevant than the previous prophetic holy visions [the New England Puritan concept of an errand in the wilderness justified by the biblical myth of exodus and conquest] was required. . . . Only a timeless story derived from the familiar, complete with plot and national hero, could yoke the diversity of the late nineteenth century and transform it into unity again" (243).

With the official government announcement in 1891 of the close of the last geographic frontier in the United States and its territories, the reality of frontier was safely placed in the realm of nostalgia, thus opening the way for its romanticization instead. Stoeltje argues that geographical, historical and cultural differences between Eastern and Western regions in the United States dramatized the frontier in regard to the geographic West, creating a synthesis of the terms "West" and "frontier."

Frederick Jackson Turner, of course, produced the most influential among the scholarly variants of the frontier myth, but Stoeltje argues that it was refined and expanded in the realm of politics, literature, and art as well, in the hands of such figures as Theodore Roosevelt, Owen Wister, and Frederick Remington, all of whom focused on the cowboy as the new hero of this new myth. Stoeltje claims the term "frontier" functions for modern America as an abbreviation for this entitling myth, in which the male Anglo Saxon hero bravely confronts the dangerous and unknown, conquering and controlling it for the use and benefit of his people.

I would argue that one reason this myth has survived and flourished over the years is that it works equally well in a postmodern context. Since the frontier itself can be seen as a set of symbols that constitute an explanation of history, it's significance as a mythic space is more important than any actual geographic location. The transfer of symbol from its place of origin to a state of unfixed, floating signifier marked the birth of American international imperialism, which began in earnest in the administration of Theodore Roosevelt. In defending his invasion of the Philippines, Roosevelt said, "I have scant patience with those who fear to undertake the task of governing the Philippines . . . but I have even scanter patience with those who make a pretense of humanitarianism to hide and cover their timidity. . . . Their doctrine, if carried out, would make it incumbent upon us to leave the Apaches of Arizona to work out their own salvation."[5] By "Indianizing" Filipino resistance to U.S. imperialism, Roosevelt was able to insinuate that what was being brought to the Filipinos, as to the Apaches of Arizona, was "salvation" and civilization, rather than conquest and exploitation, thus justifying U.S. military action at home and abroad. At the same time, he moved the now geographically defunct American frontier into a sort of turn-of-the-century cyberspace, ubiquitous but unlocatable, everywhere but nowhere in particular. The Anglo male hero could now be envisioned battling not only Apache warriors or Mexican banditos, but Filipinos, dirty japs, commie reds, Viet Cong, or, in the most recent manifestation, Arab terrorists and Muslim extremists, all in the name of American values, civilization, and democracy.

Stoeltje also maintains that this myth was created and controlled largely by and for a white male Eastern elite (a class to which Roosevelt, Wister, and Remington all belonged). I would argue, however, that at this point Stoeltje falls into a trap common to the nineteenth century, assuming an act of mythopoesis blooming in a space of superior Anglo Saxon purity, entirely unmarked by centuries of contact with Native American and Mexican cultures. Indians, Mexicans, and other non-Anglos are, as in much of Turner's thesis, virtually invisible here as active participants in the unfolding of history and the shaping of myth. They lurk in the background as shadowy figures, objects acted upon by Anglos with no more agency than trees in a forest that must be cleared to allow for white settlement. (Indeed the tying together of nature and brown-skinned Other harkens back to the earliest Puritan writings about the frontier.) Such a move is an attempt concomitantly to silence the landscape and its inhabitants and to justify the conquest and colonization of both by invoking that silence. In this version, Anglos remain uninfluenced by the voices or visions of the peoples they have conquered and whose land they inhabit, and the resulting Anglo myths appear to be purely that—Anglo.

Far from being safely and conveniently silenced, however, the myths of the non-Anglo inhabitants of the Americas reverberate through what may appear to be a singularly white narrative. The stories told by the dominant culture in America about the past and the present, the modern frontier myth through which we view ourselves and the world, are pierced with the lives, voices, and experiences of non-Anglos. Rather than a unilateral process of mythmaking, the works of the writers examined in this study illustrate the startling extent to which all our myths have become inextricably linked through the ongoing experiences of imperialism and globalization in a transformative, dialogic process.

Still, while the modern frontier myth is not lily white, neither is it free from the tension of generations of violence between the competing versions and voices that have given it breath and that continue to reimagine it today. Richard Slotkin argues that the myth of the frontier is one of Anglo regeneration through the conquest of the New World and that "the myth of regeneration through violence became the structuring metaphor" of the myth of the frontier.[6] Violence at the heart of the modern American myth, he claims, results directly from the experience of white Americans in the appropriation of Native American lands and the fascination and horror directed at Indians, Indian myths, and the ever-present reality of cultural and racial mixing.

But once the myth had moved beyond the geographic borders of the United States, as it did in the hands of Roosevelt, the savage war Slotkin identifies between whites and Indians was no longer viewed as an historical exception relevant only to the Anglo European experience in the Americas but rather as the inevitable outcome of any meeting between "civilization" and "savagery." It is on this transglobal level that history comes to operate as myth, and myth becomes the blueprint for and justification of attitudes and behaviors. The nineteenth-century narrative of the Anglo duty to defeat the savages and make the West safe for white civilization now becomes the American duty to defeat the savages and make the world safe for democracy. Nation building, regime change, and the war on terrorism have become the modern versions of civilizing the frontier, as we are asked to think mythologically about policy questions and the mission of America as global superpower.

The mission of imperialism, however, even for superpowers, can have unintended consequences. Said wrote in 1993 that "Partly because of empire, all cultures are involved in one another; none is single and pure, all are hybrid, heterogeneous, extraordinarily differentiated, and unmonolithic."[7] This is even truer today, with a McDonald's and a Starbucks on every street corner from Moscow to Mexico City, and twenty-four-hour cybercafes drawing hordes of customers in Beijing and Baghdad. In fact, in looking at the myth of the frontier through a postmodern lens, it becomes apparent that once the frontier between cultures has been breached, especially through the multiple assaults of imperialism, no space of purity remains on either side.

This is evident in the development of the frontier hero in American literature. The seventeenth- and eighteenth-century Indian-like hunter and Indian fighter of Cooper's tales, who uses an Anglo rifle but is clad in Native American buckskin, became our first hybridized mythological cultural hero, the mythical forebear of the cowboy, who, though he is projected back onto the nineteenth century, is, as Stoeltje posits, a mainly twentieth-century figure defined in large part by his violent opposition to Indians and his conquest of wild nature to which they are closely tied. And yet even this most Anglo-appearing of heroes is part Indian through his descent from that most famous Anglo frontier figure—Daniel Boone. Much of the Boone myth is in fact a hybridized version of various Native American myths.[8]

In the modern American imagination, the pervasiveness of images of the Western frontier and its heroes is so extensive even one hundred years after the official close of the frontier, those archetypes have become important building blocks in what Lauren Berlant terms the National Symbolic.[9] A tangle of legal, territorial, linguistic, and experiential forces continually at work defining the nation and the citizen, the National Symbolic is constructed through the production of National Fantasy, those "images, narratives, monuments, and sites that circulate throughout personal/collective consciousness" (5). Berlant argues that the space of the National Symbolic serves to define nationality and identity, not on the individual level, but on the level of national consciousness in the form of collective memory, popular stories, and official and unofficial histories.

In the United States, the National Symbolic is filled with fantasy images from the mythic frontier, influencing everything from film to fashion, food to literature to architecture, furniture design, and foreign policy. The permeation of these mythic images into the fabric of everyday life in the United States is so ubiquitous as to be almost invisible, and yet, as with any powerful myth, the myth of the frontier elicits deep and immediate responses in Americans. Advertisers have long put this response to profitable use. Ford Motor Company's three best-selling vehicles for nearly twenty years were the Mustang, the Pinto, and the Bronco—all distinctly Western names for horses. The Bronco has been rechristened the Explorer, joining Nissan's Pathfinder, Chevrolet's Blazer, Dodge's Ram and Dakota, Jeep's Wrangler and Cherokee, and Ford's newest and largest sport utility vehicle, the Expedition, in cashing in on America's instinctive response to the invocation of images from the frontier myth. Nissan has gone directly to the heart of the matter and simply named its newest pick-up truck the Frontier.

But the American myth of the frontier has become truly internationalized, invoking response from other cultures, as well. For many years now Marlboro cigarettes, with their distinctive cowboy spokesmen, have held the single most profitable brand name in the world, out-distancing even Coca-Cola and Disney. And in a sad irony that further illustrates the colonizing power of this myth, Marlboro cigarettes are the best-selling brand among Native Americans, who have one of the highest rates of cigarette smoking and lung cancer, and one of the lowest levels of life expectancy, of any population group in the United States.

In fact, a recent Harris poll notes that John Wayne was the "Number One Movie Star in America" as recently as 1995, years after his death.[10] Garry Wills claims this is because Wayne personified the perfect fantasy frontiersman. And like John Wayne, the iconography of the mythic West remains a potent form of National Fantasy in part because, as Dean MacCannell notes, icons mark a gap or attempt to cover a problem the symbolic order does not solve. While Slotkin claims that the frontier hero, by engaging the darkness on the other side of the border, both invokes that darkness in himself and his society and finally purges it, I would argue that the very persistence of the narrative structure and images of the frontier myth indicates its inability to purge the darkness on the other side of the border because the border has been so successfully and completely breached. The darkness can never be entirely purged, the mark of the Other never completely erased. No return to cultural purity is possible in a globalized world or on either side of a violated border. The issues and concerns associated with the frontiers of the past—colonialism, race relations, cultural and national identity, and human interactions with the natural world—far from being purged are in fact the very same that currently vex modern America. They are dark spots, so to speak, on the geography of the National Symbolic, disordered spaces still demanding to be rendered coherent through some structure of National Fantasy, some new mythic formation that will impose control and order and reconcile the violent contradictions between rhetoric and reality these issues make apparent.

American obsession with and theorizing about the West and frontiers continues both in popular culture and academia not only because of the fiercely denied continuity between past and present that Patricia Limerick discusses, but because much American thought about the frontier has been caught within the same double-bind James Clifford identifies as trapping many post-colonial theorists in "Pure Products Go Crazy." Much post-colonial theory, he claims, collapses in on itself because in a post-colonial space, there can be no return to purity. Post-colonial theorists can never entirely remove themselves from the colonizer's culture in order to critique it from the outside. They are always already at least partially insiders, marked by both the dominant and colonized cultures.

This is a blade, however, that cuts both ways. The colonizing culture is also permanently marked by the pollution of crossing forbidden borders and penetrating the frontiers of the colonized or conquered, especially in the United States, which has never achieved the "post" of post-colonial. Rather, historian Emma Pérez argues, the United States is caught in a time lag between the colonial and the post-colonial, a space she conceptualizes as the decolonial imaginary. The previously silenced voices of the colonized Others, she claims, become the negotiating spaces for the decolonizing subject.[11] The modern process of mythogenesis, and the hybridized myths it produces, illuminates this decolonizing struggle, carried out not only in the myths produced by colonized subjects but even within those of the dominant culture that has never been able to completely or permanently silence those persistent voices.

The figures therefore who cross over and move into and out of the dangerous spaces of frontiers and borderlands become mythic figures, reimagined by each new generation, altered and refigured in continuing attempts to understand both a colonial past and an imperial present in which the aftereffects of conquest, far from disappearing in 1891, continue to cast long shadows over American culture and our interactions with the rest of the world. This is part of an ongoing process of mythogenesis, the projection of the present onto the past in an attempt to, as Lauri Honko puts it, "recount how the world began, how our era started, how the goals that we strive to attain are determined and our most sacred values codified" (51). One of the goals of this study is to scrutinize the systematic production of myth in contemporary Western American fiction, especially as it relates to the genre of the Western, in order to reveal and understand the bedrock of previous myths on which it rests and the roles it plays in shaping patterns of thought, belief systems, and actions in everyday life.

Said claims that American culture is so strongly directed by the mythic narrative of the frontier that we insist all our cultural histories and stories end with a similar imagined triumph. This is evident, I would argue, in the ways we have remembered and mythologized the Japanese attack on Pearl Harbor, with white America's eventual triumph over an evil racialized Other, and in much of the rhetoric surrounding the 9/11 attacks, which are often compared to that assault. We have deliberately erased from public memory, for example, the 1900 Galveston hurricane that killed over six thousand people, claiming more lives than any other natural disaster in American history. On the other hand, every schoolchild learns about the successful fight to develop the vaccine that defeated polio, while few Americans who did not live through it have heard of the 1918 influenza epidemic that killed ten times more Americans than World War I and infected 28 percent of the U.S. population. So many young Americans died in the twenty-four months of the epidemic that the national average life span was reduced by over ten years, yet the event has virtually disappeared from cultural memory, like the Galveston hurricane incapable of being fitted into our heroic myth of national triumph. How will we eventually mythologize or forget the fight against AIDS? The attacks on the World Trade Center and the Pentagon? The war on terrorism? The threat of Saddam Hussein and the war in Iraq? It is, I think, still too soon to determine how or even if these events will enter the ongoing narrative of our national myth, or whether, like the Galveston hurricane and the influenza epidemic, they will instead be quietly deleted from our cultural memory banks. But the texts discussed here give us tantalizing clues for interpreting the rhetoric we are already invoking in our attempts to come to grips with the results of American cultural and economic imperialism.

The story of Jessica Lynch, for example, offers a particularly fascinating example of how deeply embedded in American national(ist) identity this myth is. Captivity narratives as precursor to and subgenre of the Western have always been immensely popular in the U.S., especially when they present captive white women in the hands of a savage Other. I discuss this form of the frontier myth at length in chapter 3 of this text, where I examine Leslie

Marmon Silko's novel *Ceremony* as an Indian captivity narrative. As many scholars have noted, this mythic trope becomes especially powerful in the United States during times of war, when the nation sees itself as vulnerable and under attack. The Pentagon's astonishing "spinning" of the details of Lynch's captivity and rescue, deliberately evoking exaggerated images of feminine (American) innocence and its redemption through justified violence, resulted in a massive and immediate public response. This response illustrates how powerfully the frontier myth shapes America's perception of itself as a nation and its image of itself in relation to the rest of the world.

At the same time, the story of the ambush of Lynch's unit highlights the equally astonishing postmodern twists this narrative has undergone. For perhaps the first time in U.S. history, a woman has simultaneously (and very publicly) filled the role of both brave American fighter and helpless feminine captive.[12] The nation's deeply emotional, but profoundly uneasy, response to this situation produced a national moment of cognitive dissonance—all the proper mythic signifiers were present, but some of them were in the wrong place. Ideology and myth became momentarily separated, or put another way, the ideology that myth normally makes invisible peeked through the cracks that appeared when the mythic players shifted out of their expected positions.

This became even more apparent in the nation's guiltily enthusiastic heroification of Jessica Lynch's best friend and fellow soldier, Lori Piestewa, who was killed in the ambush that resulted in Lynch's capture. Piestewa, a Hopi Indian from northern Arizona, is believed to be the first Native American woman killed in combat, as reporters stated repeatedly. But this is a carefully worded statement. More accurately, Piestewa is the first Native American woman killed while fighting for, rather than against, the U.S. military. The media, and the nation's, embrace of her (to the exclusion of the ten other soldiers from her unit who also died in the ambush) can be seen as both an affirmation of her bravery and of her safely "Americanized" identity. Like the white army recruiter who signs up Tayo and Rocky in Silko's first novel, white Americans are reassured about their cultural innocence when the descendants of people invaded and nearly exterminated to build a modern nation agree to fight and die on its behalf. None of the other soldiers killed in the ambush offered the same postmodern opportunity to (at least partially) expiate national guilt for or affirm the rightness of the savage war waged against Piestewa's ancestors. Arizona governor Janet Napolitano, with the enthusiastic support of most of the Arizona legislature, even passed a bill calling for the renaming of Squaw Peak (a prominent Phoenix landmark) and Squaw Peak Parkway (a major Phoenix thoroughfare), rechristening them Piestewa

Peak and Piestewa Parkway. While Native Americans in Arizona requested for years that all landmarks and roads in the state bearing the name "squaw" be changed, their pleas were consistently dismissed. The Hopi and their Navajo neighbors, however, traditional enemies engaged in a long-standing and bitter land dispute in the region, were united through their shared grief over the death of Piestewa and shortly afterward took the first steps in reconciling the feud that divided the tribes for decades.

By early 2004, however, national media attention had shifted elsewhere, and many legislators reversed their stand on the Squaw Peak name change, arguing Napolitano had forced it through for political reasons. Piestewa's family and other tribal members made an emotional plea on March 23, 2004 (the one-year anniversary of Piestewa's death), asking that the legislature reject two measures aimed at restoring the word "squaw" to the landmark and the freeway, which have now been officially renamed Piestewa Peak and Piestewa Freeway.

Piestewa's rise and fall in public prominence, and the political uses to which her military service has been put are a disturbing echo of the response to another famous Native American soldier from Arizona. Ira Hayes, a Pima (Tohono O'odham) Indian from the Pima (Tohono O'odham) Reservation south of Phoenix, was one of six marines caught on film struggling to raise the American flag on Iwo Jima in what is perhaps the most famous war-time photograph ever taken. It would win photographer Joe Rosenthal the Pulitzer Prize, and almost instantly would become a powerful cultural symbol of America's military triumphs on the world stage. Its image of bravery and perseverance in the face of overwhelming odds confronted in a righteous battle against racialized evil resonated perfectly with the self-image of white Ameria reflected in the rhetoric of Manifest Destiny, reifying the rightness of American military actions on domestic and foreign frontiers. Three of the six marines were killed in combat immediately after the picture was taken, but Hayes and the other two survivors were brought back to the U.S., hailed by the War Department and mass media as heroes, and shuttled from city to city to aide in the U.S. government's war bond drive. Intensely uncomfortable with this role, Hayes asked to be sent back to the front lines, saying "sometimes I wish that guy had never made that picuture."

He returned to the Pima Reservation after the end of the war a nationally famous war hero. He found, however, that the farming community's major source of water for irrigating their crops had been diverted for use by the city of Phoenix. The Reservation economy was devastated and Hayes, deeply disillusioned, began drinking heavily. Over the next ten years, as conditions on the Reservation deteriorated, Hayes would be arrested for public drunkenness nearly fifty times. In 1954, he was called to Washington, D.C. for the dedication ceremony for the cast bronze replica that had been made of the Iwo Jima photograph. Ten weeks later, in January 1955, his body was found in an irrigation ditch on the Pima Reservation. A coroner's report noted he had died of exposure after drinking heavily, stumbling into the ditch and passing out in the two inches of muddy water at its bottom, which was the sole source of water the government allotted to the Indians. Hayes was thirty-two years old at the time of his death.

The disparity between the treatment Hayes received as war hero on what became known as the Bond Tour—meeting with the president, signing autographs, being feted by the press—and the distinctly different Indian reality to which he returned on his Reservation underscores the racial character of the hero in the savage war. While a nonwhite person may fill the role for a time, especially if his or her heroism seems to reassure white America of its cultural innocence, once the mantle of war hero is removed, that of subaltern "Other" replaces it. This becomes especially evident in looking at the figure of the captive woman in the frontier myth.

Her necessary whiteness is made apparent in the American public's lack of enthusiasm in its response to another of Lynch's fellow soldiers also captured after the ambush. Shoshana Johnson, an African American woman, was shot through both legs during the firefight and held by the Iraqis for twenty-two days, along with five other soldiers from the unit. (Lynch, whose horrific injuries were caused when the Humvee she was riding in overturned during the attack, was held for eight days). Despite being videotaped by her captors, thus providing a seemingly perfect vehicle for presentation by the media, Shoshana Johnson received relatively little press coverage after her release and has virtually disappeared from the national radar screen, while Jessica Lynch received a reported one million dollars from the New York publisher Knopf to write the story of her life, which was published in 2003 as *I'm a Soldier, Too: The Jessica Lynch Story.* Her narration thus enters the stream of the national narration, reifying through the mythic form it assumed, the larger myth of America as a frontier nation, and the postmodern frontier myth as a now truly globalized phenomenon.

This study examines the process of contemporary mythmaking as it is carried out in the novels of three Western writers in order to illuminate the process of the reconstruction of the past, the reimagining of history, and the revisioning of the future, especially as these processes take place within, or directly challenge, the genre of the Western. I decided that a close examination of a small number of relatively representative writers would be more revealing than a quick survey of many. I begin therefore with an interrogation of the works of an author most commonly believed to reflect those themes, values, and symbols found in traditional frontier myths, a writer who is arguably one of the most controversial and problematic authors on the American literary scene. Cormac McCarthy has been accused of sexism for not creating more female characters, of racism for writing mainly about Anglos, and of romanticizing violent, politically incorrect cowboys. He has been seen by many as the prototypical white male Western writer, a sort of modern-day Owen Wister with a heavy dose of Faulknerian Southern Gothic and as an agent propagating American imperial expansionism.

I chose him in part because he is an Anglo male who writes from the perspective most commonly associated with the histories, stories, and myths about American frontiers in the popular imagination. Yet he savagely subverts the very myths he evokes so lovingly. Like Joseph Conrad, he both reproduces and critiques imperial ideology, at once problematizing and romanticizing traditional tropes in a complexly postmodern vision of a future tied with bonds of blood to the legacy of the mythic past. His voice and the frontier heroes he creates are both a continuance of the tradition of Western writing and a dark and complex counterpoint to it.

Leslie Marmon Silko also insists on the troubling connections among past, present, and future, tracing the tangled threads of Native American, Mexican, and Anglo stories about themselves and each other and prophesying an apocalyptic, blood-washed future in which all myths feed off the flesh of the others. Like McCarthy's, her new vision is both ancient—constructed of traditional Pueblo, Navajo, Mayan, Mexican, and Anglo myths—and postmodern—a terrifying, ever-shifting vision of races mixed by rape and identities raped by mixing. Even more emphatically than McCarthy, Silko draws the themes and consequences of her myth across national borders and into a globalized nightmare.

As a Native American woman, Silko might seem at first glance to stand in sharp contrast to McCarthy, and indeed I felt an Indian perspective absolutely necessary to this study. I decided on Silko for several reasons. Partly because I felt a woman's voice was also necessary, partly because she writes from and about the same region as McCarthy, and also because, like McCarthy, her works range from past to present to prophetic future, insisting on the power of myths to shape all three. The myths that inform her work are themselves sprung from multiple traditions and backgrounds and indeed exultant in their hybridity. The connections between the sometimes competing, sometimes complimentary visions of these two writers, especially as they converge on the body of the mythic hero operating within the space of a postmodern frontier, are especially telling.

Ana Castillo's mythic vision of a borderlands utopia, while marginally less violent than McCarthy's or Silko's, is nonetheless a myth of bloody birth, a sorrow-tinged Eden born from the tragic deaths and mutilated bodies of Chicanas. Harkening back to the sacred tales of medieval Europe and shaped by the myths of Pueblo and Mexican cultures, Castillo's Southwestern utopia is created from battles fought by the poor, the brown-skinned, and the marginalized, who refuse the simple martyrdom of the original European myth for a more complex, postmodern version in which utopia must be paid for in blood, and the martyred saints are strangers to the church.

Like McCarthy, Castillo is an immigrant to the West, the Chicago-born daughter of immigrants from Mexico. Bilingual, multicultural, her common American identity of mixed worlds and crossed borders is one reason the frontier myth, a story inherently about mixing and crossing, remains this country's defining metaphor and the blueprint for our cultural identity. While Rudolfo Anaya, for instance, writes about the West as someone born and raised in the region, and while his work is certainly deeply mythic, I felt that Castillo's texts, centered on the journey from one place to another in a utopic quest, spoke even more profoundly to the realities and the myths that have shaped the modern West and modern America.

The spaces in which the works of these three writers collide offer some sharply differentiated visions, but the spaces in which overlap has occurred, where the myths of one culture have become inextricably, often unknowingly, intertwined with those of another, each forcing the others into new and unsuspected forms, provide the most startling insights. Sometimes beautiful, sometimes tragic, the new myths born from these couplings are nonetheless, like any living story, the expressions of the larger culture from which they spring, both a projection onto a troubled and troubling past and an insistent, prophetic vision of a shared future.

My hope is that readers and critics of this book will use it to further lines of inquiry and argument into the roles of history and myth as active agents in the shaping of modern cultures, to further interrogate the relationships between them, and to examine the changing forms of myth emerging from current cultural and political struggles, identity politics, and increasingly challenged assumptions about the roles and realities of racial, ethnic, and national borders in a globalized world.

CHAPTER 1

Foundation of Empire

The Sacred Hunter and the Eucharist of the Wilderness in Cormac McCarthy's *Blood Meridian*

> *The Foundation of Empire is Art and Science. Remove them or Degrade them and the Empire is No more. Empire follows Art and not vice verse.*
>
> WILLIAM BLAKE

Cormac McCarthy's Southwestern works, and *Blood Meridian* in particular, have been seen as both archetypal Westerns and as anti-Westerns, as myth and counter-myth, as glorifications of American imperialism and as damning indictments of it. I will argue here that McCarthy does indeed evoke archetypal myths and mythic heroes that have traditionally been used to serve the cause of American westward expansion and imperialism. That is, in part, the function of myth—to legitimate current social structures through a stylized vision of the past, to offer blueprints for behaviors and attitudes, and to justify future actions. I will also argue, however, that by uncovering the most ancient bones underlying these myths and using them to construct a new mythic vision of history, McCarthy is deliberately deconstructing the imperialist aims and justifications of the old myths while disrupting assumptions about the ideas and identities they were intended to uphold. The result is indeed an indictment, bloody and accusatory, of an American national(ist) identity based on the violent conquest of both racialized Others and feminized nature. The new mythic vision presented in *Blood Meridian* offers a postmodern challenge to notions of essentialized ethnic and national identities and borders.

One of the many complex relationships McCarthy explores in *Blood Meridian, or, The Evening Redness in the West* is between humans, especially Anglo Americans, and the natural world. He does so in part through the manipulation of several archetypal myths closely identified with the European experience in the New World, tracing their collapse and rebirth in the border regions of the American Southwest. McCarthy moves *Blood Meridian* through the dark and disordered spaces of what Lauren Berlant terms the National Symbolic, but unlike the familiar icons of mythic frontier tales, McCarthy's characters seek no closure, nor do they render order out of the chaos of history. Rather, they reveal the chaos at the heart of history and the myths we make from it. The novel functions on the level of myth-making and National Fantasy as an American origin story, a reimaging upon the palimpsest of the Western frontier the birth of one of our most pervasive National Fantasies—the winning of the West and the building of the American character through frontier experiences.[1]

Both of these related themes demand a wilderness to be conquered, either literally via ax and plow or metaphorically by defeating the Indians rhetorically tied to the wild landscape. Annette Kolodny has defined the American obsession with land, especially land-as-woman, as an American Pastoral, drawing some images from the European version, yet unique from it. The literary hero within this landscape, she says, is "the lone male in the wilderness" (*The Lay of the Land*, 147) struggling to define a relationship with the female landscape in its troubling metaphorical appearance as both fruitful mother and untouched virgin, one image offering nurturing fertility while the other demands penetration and conquest.

Blood Meridian chronicles the origin of this figure, sometimes called the American Adam, though not the benignly patriarchal John Wayne version. McCarthy's project is not simply to retell the familiar myths or dress up the icons of cowboys and Indians in modern, politically correct costumes. Rather he is using the trope of the historic frontier and the landscape of the Southwest within the genre of the Western to interrogate the consequences of our acceptance of archetypal Western hero myths. *Blood Meridian* rewrites and reorders those myths in such a way as to bridge the discontinuity Patricia Limerick identifies as being perceived by the public to exist between the mythic past of the American West and its modern realities.[2] This gap, marked by the feeling of discontinuity and limned by continued popular obsession with traditional Western and frontier icons that have thus far failed to cover it, is filled in *Blood Meridian* with a newly structured version of National Fantasy, though not one that imposes any kind of hoped-for order or control.

Instead McCarthy presents a counter-memory, a sort of anti-myth of the West, illuminating especially the roots of the modern American relationships between Anglos and non-Anglos and between humans and the natural world. In many ways McCarthy has produced a counter-history, in contradiction to the meaning generated from most official histories of the period. It is within the accuracy of the historical detail of *Blood Meridian* that McCarthy finds his mythic history, lurking within the liminal spaces of the familiar rhetoric of Manifest Destiny, the taming of the wilderness, John Wayne's famous swagger, and other pillars of the National Symbolic.

Kolodny argues that the American Pastoral was structured around the yeoman farmer responding to the female landscape and discusses this figure as he appears in Jefferson, Crevecoeur, Freneau, and others. However, as Henry Nash Smith notes, the image of the yeoman farmer was simply not romantic enough to sustain popular interest for long. What emerged instead was an American version of a far older figure—the hunter—that existed in both European and Native American myths.

The myth of the sacred hunter, as Richard Slotkin explains it, is one of regeneration through violence enacted upon the body of the earth. The hunter must leave the safety of his community, track his game (usually a representation of the spirit of the wilderness or an avatar of a nature deity), and slay it. In many versions, both Native American and European, the prey allows itself to be hunted and killed, willingly sacrificing its life to sustain the life of the hunter and his community, who must in turn give honor and thanks to the prey and to whichever nature spirit it represents. Following the hunt, he and/or his community either literally or symbolically consume the prey in a eucharist of the wilderness, thus renewing the hunter and providing life for those he serves. The eucharist, Slotkin says, is itself a sublimation of the myth of the sacred marriage that enacts a sexual union between the hunter and the body of nature. The game the hunter tracks in many versions of this myth is revealed at the end of the chase to be some female representative of the wilderness whom the hunter marries, instead of slaying, in a parallel renewal of self and community through sexual union with nature.[3]

Slotkin writes that, in the Anglo American version, "The hunter myth provided a fictive justification for the process by which the wilderness was to be expropriated and exploited" (554). It did so by seeing that process in terms of heroic male adventure commodified by visual and symbolic proofs of the hunter's heroic stature and, therefore, his rightful and proper triumph over his prey. The famous image of Davy Crockett standing proudly next to his stack of 150 bearskins, the legend of Paul Bunyon clearing miles of virgin forest with a single stroke of his ax, and the often-photographed mountains of buffalo skulls towering over the Great Plains embody this version of the myth.

The vision of a feminine landscape within the patriarchal bounds of Anglo American culture and the long-standing tradition of associating Native Americans with what appeared to early Anglo colonists as a "howling wilderness" both encouraged and justified this exploitation. In *Blood Meridian* these images are echoed in the scalphunters' collections of scalps, ears, teeth, and various other trophies, as well as described in detail on the plain of the bone pickers. What is echoed and amplified as well is the subtle shift evident in the modern Anglo version of the myth, from the imaging of the prey as symbol of divine nature sacrificed so that man may live, to simply that which deserves to fall before him.

The gigantic figure of Judge Holden, who is both a fictional version of an historical personage and an amalgamation of numerous archetypes from the mythic West, acts throughout the book as the author of the new version of the hunter myth. McCarthy consistently presents the judge as a priest, a mediator between man and nature, shepherding, or more accurately manipulating, the scalphunters' souls even as Glanton guides their physical bodies. The image of the judge as priest is consistent with the dominant mood and tone of *Blood Meridian* as origin myth—a sacred tale recounting how the world came to be. Bernard Schopen calls the entire novel "profoundly religious" and claims it takes place "in a physical and thematic landscape charged with religious nuance, allusion, and language" (191). That is not to say that *Blood Meridian* is a Christian book or particularly interested in presenting any kind of Christian worldview. At its deepest structural and rhetorical levels, *Blood Meridian* utilizes mythic and religious imagery both Christian and non-Christian in order to strip away the layers of blind belief myths compel.

The judge, a mythic figure in his own right, is the terrifying guide to the disintegration of the last vestiges of the old sacred hunter myth and its rebirth as the modern myth of the American frontier. The first time we see the judge is at the revival meeting tent where the primary charge he levels against the apparently innocent Reverend Green foreshadows the betrayal and perversion he will commit as the novel progresses. The minister, the judge claims, is wanted "On a variety of charges the most recent of which involved a girl of eleven years—I said eleven—who had come to him in trust and whom he was surprised in the act of violating while actually clothed in the livery of his God" (7). This violation of a child and the profaning of a sacred office by the figure entrusted with upholding and protecting it will be enacted again and again throughout the novel with the judge playing the leading role.

The judge deliberately cultivates a feel for myth, ritual, and religion and directs it toward his own ends. His goal is to harness the unconscious response to mythic heroes, invoke it with the rituals of the sacred hunter and the eucharist of the wilderness, and reorder, or perhaps disorder, it on a deep and essential level. The result is a new myth that restructures American attitudes and beliefs about what it means to be an American and how Americans must relate to the landscape they inhabit.

Throughout *Blood Meridian* the judge both exalts the natural world and strives to contain and destroy it, to usurp its power for his own ends. He is priest here, not only of men's souls, but of their minds as well, and he often appears as the spokesman of what is presented as a sort of new religion—science. As the novel progresses the figure of the judge becomes more and more godlike, while that of nature is debased. The judge manipulates the power and mystery of the natural world and its association with the sacred through his scientific knowledge, which gives him the ability to penetrate that mystery and therefore disrupt the assumptions of the other characters about the place of humans within the world. As the scalphunters are camped at an abandoned mine, the judge collects ore samples

> in whose organic lobations he purported to read news of the earth's origins. . . . A few would quote him scripture to confound his ordering up of eons out of the ancient chaos and other apostate supposings. The judge smiled.
>
> Books lie, he said.
>
> God dont lie.
>
> No, said the judge. He does not. And these are his words.
>
> He held up a chunk of rock.
>
> He speaks in stones and trees, the bones of things.
>
> The squatters in their rags nodded among themselves and were soon reckoning him correct . . . and this the judge encouraged until they were right proselytes of the new order whereupon he laughed at them for fools. (116)

The acceptance of traditional Christian dogma regarding the world and the place of man in the natural order of existence is deconstructed by the judge, built anew through the acceptance and belief of his listeners, then destroyed again. His audience now doubts their own understanding of nature as well as Christian doctrine, but the one figure whose personal power has increased in the eyes of his followers is Judge Holden. The judge is laying groundwork, gathering "proselytes," participants in the ritualistic myth he is enacting.

That nature plays the part of the sacred does not imply the sort of patriarchal relationship imagined by Christianity in which a merciful, all-powerful God cares for and watches over his children. As many have noted, in McCarthy's work nature is often brutal and almost always without mercy for humans, and yet the shadow of the sacred and the profane permeates *Blood Meridian* and is constantly evoked by the judge through man's relationship to the natural world. That this destructive version of the myth he is bringing to fruition demands material evidence of its fulfillment does not lessen its ritualistic power. The judge, having symbolically dethroned the priest of the Christian rituals and myths at the revival tent, will make proselytes of the scalphunters and lead them in a cannibalistic perversion of the old myth made new in this place where "not again in all the world's turning will there be terrains so wild and barbarous to try whether the stuff of creation may be shaped to man's will or whether his own heart is not another kind of clay" (5).

Whether the stuff of creation may be shaped to man's will, I would argue, is one of the central questions of the novel, implicating American attitudes regarding man's conquest of nature, the relationship of Anglo America to any non-Anglo peoples, and America's imperial mission especially as it was imagined in relation to the West. Dana Phillips claims that what McCarthy is questioning is "whether human beings have any privileged position in relation to the rest of the world" (443). His answer is that, according to McCarthy, they do not. Humans and nature are simply part of the same continuum, mutually ignoring each other throughout the novel. At first glance it would seem that indeed creation *cannot* be shaped to man's will, or, as Phillips says, "at least not for very long. Man's will does not seem a very relevant or potent force in this novel" (439). However, a closer examination suggests that in fact man's will is the most potent of forces as well as the central concern in the terrifying relationship between Holden and the kid. It is man's will that ultimately shapes myth, and, McCarthy implies, it is our myths that also ultimately shape the world. The agent of this shaping is not nature but Judge Holden who, as the only character who truly understands the immense power of will, acts almost as collective human will made flesh in order to shape the stuff of creation through the shaping of the myth that constructs it.

Phillips would likely disagree with this interpretation. He argues that there is no inherent meaning in the actions of the characters or of the natural world in *Blood Meridian*, that darkness is just darkness, death just death. McCarthy has even "dispensed with the concept of character" (441) in the traditional sense, Phillips says, in order to erase any hint of possible moral redemption for his band of scalphunters and their victims. I would argue, however, that the lack of traditional character development by McCarthy is more than a response to the "furious troping" (441) of Melville's Ishmael or an avoidance of Flannery O'Connor–style moralizing. McCarthy is interested in myths, not morals. It is true, as Phillips notes, that there are no real surprises in the plot of *Blood Meridian,* that "all the novel's complexities are fully present from the first page. . . . The novel does not seek to resolve 'conflicts' which trouble its characters" (443). This is so, not because there is no meaning or symbolism in the world of *Blood Meridian,* but because, like any mythic story, we already know the outcome. The characters are not explored in the Lukacsian sense because, as actors in a myth, their individualities are less important than the roles they are playing. The face of the hero is infinitely changeable; therefore the kid does not need a proper name, Judge Holden can be endowed with faculties that border on the superhuman, and Tobin can be referred to as simply "expriest" as often as he is called by name. Meaning resides solely in the actions the characters take and the power of their story to shape the world of those who hear it.

It is true that the Christian god and the moral structures he represents are absent in the natural world of *Blood Meridian,* at least as a cipherable entity to the travelers. The judge alone among the scalphunters claims the power to solve the mysteries of the natural world, and he does so through science and a skewed rationality cloaked with the rhetoric of religion. The myth of science, with the judge as its sacred high priest, is opposed to the earlier myth of nature served by the sacred hunter. Within the space of the National Symbolic and in the tradition of the earliest Puritan writings about the New World, the judge's figuring of wilderness as that which must be conquered by man lest it conquer him is a familiar trope, common to virtually every Western written after the mid-nineteenth century.

Kolodny argues this is part of the defining structure of the American Pastoral, born in conjunction with the first stirrings of the Industrial Revolution, that "implicit in the metaphor of the land-as-woman was both the regressive pull of maternal containment *and* the seductive invitation to sexual assertion" (67). Henry Nash Smith notes that by the late 1850s, as the myth of the garden and the land as fruitful mother began to fray, the archetypal frontier hero in the American wilderness had lost Leatherstocking's "power to commune with nature. . . . He no longer looks to God through nature, for nature is no longer benign: its symbols are the wolves and the prairie fire . . . . The landscape within which the Western hero operates has become . . . 'a dreary waste.' . . . He is . . . alone in a hostile, or at best a neutral, universe" (89). And yet the relationship McCarthy explores is considerably more complex than the simple nihilism of "Nature does not care for man."

Dana Phillips refutes Vereen Bell's claim that human beings and nature compete in the novel by arguing that "this competition has been decided in favor of . . . the natural world even before *Blood Meridian* begins" (446). Humans and the natural world are not antagonists, Phillips claims, but are instead "parts of the same continuum" (446). That is indeed the case at the outset of the novel, and the balance of power between the various parts of the continuum appears fairly equal, but it is the fundamental change in this relationship, enacted on the level of the mythic and sacred, that McCarthy is interested in uncovering. That the nature of that relationship exists on a level significantly deeper than mutual indifference or antagonism is clear. Again and again, McCarthy invokes archetypal myths and references to the sacred when portraying humans in the natural world. Travelers of all sorts in the wilderness are commonly referred to as "pilgrims" and "proselytes." As the scalphunters cross a dry lakebed, the narrator claims that the earth itself notes their passing, "As if the very sediment of things contained yet some residue of sentience. As if in the transit of those riders were a thing so profoundly terrible as to register even to the uttermost granulation of reality" (247). The narrator continues with the often-quoted passage regarding the quality of light in the desert that "bequeathed a strange equality and no one thing nor spider nor stone nor blade of grass could put forth claim to precedence. . . . and in the optical democracy of such landscapes all preference is made whimsical and a man and a rock become endowed with unguessed kinships" (247). These passages have often been interpreted as "a critique of our culture's anthropocentrism,"[4] and, as Phillips notes, "the human does not stand out among the other beings and objects that make up the world" (443). However, that relationship of indifferent equanimity is neither stable nor unchanging. It is the laying bare of the cataclysmic evolution taking place in the mythic formations that have created this structure that McCarthy seeks to document through the actions of his characters and their mythic roles.

If we view the relationship between man and nature in *Blood Meridian* in terms of the sacred hunter myth, a clear set of images appears. This myth implies the necessity of a certain kind of relationship between man and nature—a bloody and violent one to be sure and one that does not necessarily hold any moral overtones in the Christian sense of right or wrong or good or evil, but simply a set of rules governing what is, how reality and the natural world work, and a sense of order and balance in the roles of each. That, of course, is the most basic function of myth, to organize and impose order upon man and his world, though in *Blood Meridian* the revelation of the profound disorder at the heart of our myths seems to be the ultimate goal.

The scalphunters as a group can be read as playing the part of the sacred hunter, dark versions of classic Western heroes from the Deerslayer and Daniel Boone to Buffalo Bill, leaving their communities to enter the wilderness for renewal and regeneration through the act of hunting and killing. Although the scalphunters seek a human prey, it is a prey nonetheless rhetorically tied to the wilderness, and the goal of its killing is ostensibly the protection and renewal of the scalphunters' foster community—the Mexicans living in Sonora. And yet the fact that their prey *is* human begins the degeneration of the myth, tilts it off its axis. Of course the epigraph from the *Yuma Daily Sun* that opens the novel (detailing a 300,000-year-old skull found in the Afar region of Ethiopia that showed evidence of having been scalped) implies that such a perversion is equally as old as the myth itself. This idea is furthered by the name of the judge's gun, "Et in Arcadia Ego" (Even in Arcadia am I [Death]) implying as Leo Daugherty notes that "the point of the gun's name is not that because of its appearance in the landscape, or by synecdoche the judge's appearance, death has been introduced into an idyllic Arcadia: the entire novel makes clear (primarily through the judge, who continuously emphasizes the point in his preachments) that the human world is, and has always been, a world of killing" (126–27).

The figure of the judge within this space is a Conradian expression of white American civilization, or perhaps the brutal force of its will. Like Kurtz, the judge engages in a savage war that is both sanctioned and denied by various authorities; like Kurtz he carries his war forward from both sides, existing at once as the ultimate expression of Euro-American manhood (poet/scholar/warrior) and as the primitive savage he seeks to destroy and emulate, donning native clothing and defeating native peoples on their own ground. And more importantly, like Kurtz, the judge is the agent of the revelation of the savagery at the heart of the myth and the civilization that produces it. Once the prey of the sacred hunter becomes human, imperialism itself becomes a sacred act, mythically justified by the very narrative on which it depends.

Through the course of the novel, the judge will turn the old myth on its head, pervert it and cannibalize it. He leads the scalphunters in acts that violate the relationship contained within the sacred hunter myth while still seeming to follow its internal rules, in the same way the Black Mass was seen as an inversion of a sacred ritual and indeed depended on the sacred nature of the original for its own symbolic power. This degeneration of the myth from within sounds a striking note of prophecy, for it marks a change not only in the outer form of the hero and his universe (to be expected as cultures change with the passage of time), but also in the most basic narrative structure of the myth. A change on this level, Slotkin claims, "reflect(s) a fundamental alteration of the culture's conception of the relationship of man to the universe, a revolution in world view, cosmology, historical and moral theory, and self-concept. Hence such changes may be seen as marking the point at which a new epoch of cultural history or perhaps even a new culture can be said to begin" (*Regeneration through Violence*, 9). The neobiblical rhetoric of the novel and its blood-washed, apocalyptic images support this vision of revolution, of violent death and rebirth, of some enormous and profound change in the fabric of things imagined by McCarthy through the perversion of the sacred hunter and his position in the natural world.

In fact the first description in the novel of Glanton and his gang mark them equally as actors within the myth and as deviants from it, as both hunters and cannibals:

> a pack of visciouslooking humans mounted on unshod indian ponies . . . bearded, barbarous, clad in the skins of animals stitched up with thews and armed with weapons of every description . . . the trappings of their horses fashioned out of human skin and their bridles woven up from human hair and decorated with human teeth and the riders wearing scapulars or necklaces of dried and blackened human ears . . . the horses rawlooking and wild in the eye and their teeth bared like feral dogs . . . the whole like a visitation from some heathen land where they and others like them fed on human flesh. Foremost among them . . . rode the judge. (78)

The natural order of the original myth governing the relationship between humans and nature has been upset so profoundly that even the horses are seen as feral, feeding on flesh instead of grass, and the hunters themselves a visitation of the profane rather than the sacred. Although Glanton is their nominal leader, it is the judge who is "foremost among them." Their sacred nature as hunter heroes is evidenced by the "scapulars" they wear and yet their pollution is obvious as well. The scapulars are formed of scores of human ears collected as trophies in the same skewed capitalistic spirit as Davy Crockett's bearskins or Paul Bunyan's logs, and indeed the native people to whom those ears belonged are viewed by the scalphunters more as natural resources than human beings, just another part of an infinitely exploitable landscape. Inevitably, however, the cannibalization at the heart of the new myth will become reified.

The first instance of the judge's symbolic cannibalization of those whom he is engaged to serve occurs when the scalphunters spend the night with the doomed miners at the ruined mines. As the gang prepares to retire for the night, "Someone had reported the judge naked atop the walls, immense and pale in the revelations of lightning, striding the perimeter up there and declaiming in the old epic mode" (118). The next morning the body of the boy is discovered, lying naked and face down, while the judge is seen "standing in the gently steaming quiet picking his teeth with a thorn as if he had just eaten" (118). The sacred marriage and the sacred eucharist in this scene are at once conflated and perverted, the whole echoing and reimagining the sacred hunter myth as well as the Christian crucifixion and eucharist.[5] The naked body of the innocent child "whose head hung straight down" (119) when the miners grabbed his arms and lifted him, mimics the image of the body of the innocent and sinless Christ on the cross, drooping head ringed by a crown of thorns. As the judge watches these procedures, he employs a thorn with which to pick his teeth clean of the cannibalized flesh of the child.

The connotations of rape in the explicit nakedness of the judge and the murdered boy mock the fertility rite of the sacred marriage with a union that produces only violence and death in much the same way as the cannibalism implied by the judge picking his teeth "as if he had just eaten" mocks the intention of renewal and life in the ritual of the eucharist. The judge both literally and symbolically consumes that which is forbidden, the child as a living representation of the community the sacred hunter is bound to serve and protect. The boy is neither proper prey for the hunter nor a proper bride, and yet as the myth is inverted and turned in upon itself he becomes both. His childlike state—weak, helpless, and lost in the wilderness—at once feminizes him and marks him as prey for the foremost hunter in the gang. In the proper fulfillment of this emerging version of the myth, the judge rapes and cannibalizes him, absorbs his essence and emerges renewed. Indeed the entire gang appears rejuvenated, associated here with the symbols of life and rebirth as the narrator tells us: upon discovery of the boy's body they "mounted up and turned their horses to the gates that now stood open to the east to welcome in the light and to invite their journey" (119).

This sequence of actions, enacting the ritual of the hunt culminating in a perversion of the sacred marriage and sacred eucharist and the regeneration of the hunters ends chapter 9. The next major action within the narrative begins in chapter 10 with the expriest Tobin relating to the kid the story of how he first met Judge Holden, a story that again involves the judge as priest leading a group of men in the perversion of the ritual of the sacred marriage.

This narrative establishes the ritualistic heart of the judge's new myth, for Tobin's story shows the gang's initiation into their roles as sacred, or perhaps profane, hunters. It is important, therefore, that McCarthy have this tale originate from one labeled "expriest," fallen from the symbolic orders, both Christian and non-Christian, of the past, and ripe therefore to be baptized into the order (or disorder) to come.

Tobin relates the much-talked-about scene in which the judge appears, alone in the middle of the desert, acting as savior for Glanton and his riders who are without gunpowder and in a desperate flight from nearly a hundred Apaches. The judge uses an uncanny knowledge of the natural landscape to lead them on a new course to a distant mountain range that holds both a bat cave full of nitre and a sulfur-ringed volcano. Tobin recalls that the judge, before commencing his bloody ritual, tells the men "that our mother the earth . . . was round like an egg and contained all good things within her. Then he turned and led the horse he had been riding across that terrain . . . and us behind him like the disciples of a new faith" (130).

And like all converts, the men are required to unite in a group ritual pledging themselves to this "new faith," legitimizing the degeneration of the myth they have been enacting all along. The judge combines charcoal, the nitre from the bat cave, and sulphur scraped from the mouth of the volcano as Tobin continues, "I didn't know but what we'd be required to bleed into it" (131). The scalphunters do pour forth their own bodies, in the form of urine instead of blood, into the hole in the earth the judge has made for the preparation of his eucharist.

> He worked it up dry with his hands and all the while the savages down there on the plain drawin nigh to us and when I turned back the judge was standin, the great hairless oaf, and he'd took out his pizzle and he was pissin into the mixture, pissin with a great vengeance and one hand aloft and he cried out for us to do likewise. . . . We hauled forth our members and at it we went and the judge on his knees kneadin the mass with his naked arms and the piss was splashin about and he was cryin out to us to piss, man, piss for your very souls for cant you see the redskins yonder, and laughin the while and workin up this great mass in a foul black dough, a devil's batter by the stink of it and him not a bloody dark pastryman himself. (132)

Here again the sacred marriage and the eucharist of the wilderness contained within both the hunter myth and Christianity are conflated and perverted.

Rather than the flesh of a deer or the sacred host, the judge kneads "a foul black mass, a devil's batter" made of elements of the natural world turned black and stinking by symbolic and ritualistic violence, with the men gang-raping the great vaginal hole in "our mother the earth," spewing piss instead of semen. The ritual reaches its violent climax with Glanton firing his rifle, primed with the foul mixture, straight down the open mouth of the volcano. The flesh of men and the flesh of nature are united here by science to birth gunpowder used to slaughter every last Apache, with the judge as a midwife and anti-priest. As the final ceremonial step cementing the men to the judge as their spiritual leader within this version of the myth, the judge "called us all about to fill our horns and flasks, and we did, one by one, circlin past him like communicants" (134). And indeed communicants are precisely what the scalphunters are, participants in a ritual of renewal dependent upon acts of violence and the perversion of the very myth (and mother) that gave them birth.

This scene, with its savage rape of the earth and resultant "butchery" (134) of the Indians, is a brilliant condensation of McCarthy's violent counter-memory of the winning of the West, his anti-myth of the frontier, deconstructing the forms of National Fantasy so often and so fondly used in building the space of the National Symbolic and shaping the attitudes that would come to justify American devastation of the natural world, genocide of native peoples, and imperial adventures from South America to Southeast Asia. Here we see that indeed "the stuff of creation may be shaped to man's will" (5). The results of the shaping, of the wholesale acceptance of this version of the sacred hunter as the governing myth of the new nation, are played out through the last half of the novel.

Immediately following this narrative, in revenge or perhaps fulfillment of the perversion of the sacred marriage/eucharist, a bear, a powerful symbol of the natural world for McCarthy, steals a Delaware. Like many chapters, this one begins with a detailed description of the natural world through which the scalphunters ride, this time the aspen and pine forests of a high mountain. The bear rises up unexpectedly beside the trail and is shot by Glanton. "The ball struck the bear in the chest and the bear leaned with a strange moan and seized the Delaware and lifted him from the horse. . . . the man dangling from the bear's jaws looked down at them cheek and jowl with the brute and one arm about its neck like some crazed defector in a gesture of defiant camaraderie" (137). Acting as an avatar of the natural world, perhaps as nature's own sacred hunter, the bear escapes with his "hostage" (137). The relationship between them is something more than simply an unlucky rider falling prey to a random wild beast or indifferent nature. The Delaware has been consumed by the myth, as the narrator states, "The bear had carried off their kinsman like some fabled storybook beast and the land had swallowed them up beyond all ransom or reprieve" (138).

By this time all the scalphunters have been swallowed up beyond ransom or reprieve by the anti-myth they are enacting, their disconnection from the wilderness through which they ride so complete that even their shadows on the stones appear "like shapes capable of violating their covenant with the flesh that authored them and continuing autonomous across the naked rock without reference to sun or man or god" (139). The balance of power, which may be perceived as resting on the side of nature at the start of the novel, has by the final scenes shifted to the side of man. The original covenant has been violated, the sacred myths structuring the relationship of man to the natural world now perverted to an extent that McCarthy suggests cannot be redeemed, reprieved, or corrected.

The first powerful vision we receive of the results of this reordered myth is on the plain of the bone pickers, fifteen years after the main action of the novel. The kid, now a man, camps on the prairie where he meets an old hunter who tells him of the slaughter of the buffalo herds in which he had participated, an event Tom Pilkington calls "an ecological calamity so stunning as to be almost inconceivable" (317). Initially the old hunter paints pictures that, while bloody and full of gore, reflect the sheer abundance of life that once existed on the now empty and silent plains: "animals by the thousands and tens of thousands and the hides pegged out over actual square miles of ground . . . and the meat rotting on the ground and the air whining with flies and the buzzards and ravens and the night a horror of snarling and feeding with the wolves half crazed and wallowing in the carrion. . . . On this ground alone there was eight million carcasses" (317). In contrast to this, the hunter then recalls the "last hunt" in which he and the other hunters searched the empty plains for six weeks for a sign of buffalo. "Finally found a herd of eight animals and we killed them and come in. They're gone. Ever one of them that God ever made is gone as if they'd never been at all" (317).

Here is the new covenant, this hunter and those like him proselytes of the new order the judge has helped bring into being in which man's relationship to the wilderness is one of butchery on a scale scarcely imaginable. The outcome is not regeneration, since no animals remain alive to carry on the relationship. This new version of the ancient hunter myth represents degeneration signified by the images of the enormous mountains of bones, miles long, stretching across the prairies in which the mythic figure of the sacred hunter has been reduced to that of the bonepickers, ragged children gathering dead evidence of the now-vanished herds. It is the logical culmination of the task the judge has set for himself early on, when Toadvine questions his taxidermy of one of every species of bird they have encountered. The judge replies, "Only nature can enslave man and only when the existence of each last entity is routed out and made to stand naked before him will he be properly suzerain of the earth. . . . The freedom of birds is an insult to me. I'd have them all in zoos" (198).

While the judge may be clothing it in the sacred rhetoric of the religion of science, we see that the will of man, far from being insignificant, is the most powerful force in the novel. If only nature can enslave man, conversely only man can enslave nature, even if by doing so he leaves a sky as empty of birds as the plains now are of buffalo. Through his will man can make himself suzerain of the earth, though in so doing he must destroy that which he would rule. Kolodny has identified this as "the pastoral paradox" and argues it is at the heart of the modern American relationship to the natural world. Within this paradox, she writes, "man might, indeed, win mastery over the landscape, but only at the cost of emotional and psychological separation from it" (*The Lady of the Land,* 28). And driven by the inexorable force of myth, man is incapable of stopping, his actions governed, directed, and justified by the myth his own deeds have reified.

This situation has been foreshadowed by the judge through the allegory he relates at the Anasazi ruins: "The father dead has euchred the son out of his patrimony" (145). In destroying the sacred power of nature and the myth that tied man to it, the father has robbed those sons to come of their right to take part in that myth and of the regeneration and rebirth to be had from it. Instead, ironically, by making himself suzerain, the hunter-father engenders his own demise, and thus has ensured that for the son, "The world which he inherits bears him false witness. He is broken before a frozen god and he will never find his way" (145). Like the son in the story, these sons will grow to be "killers of men" (145) rather than sacred hunters, resulting in generations of those "not yet born who shall have cause to curse the Dauphin's soul" (327).

And in fulfillment of the judge's desired containment of birds, the great patrimony of nature has been reduced to the level of a zoo or circus by the final chapter of the novel. The gigantic figure of the bear, formerly the magnificent and terrible avatar of the wilderness able to pluck a Delaware from the midst of the scalphunters, is now dressed in a tutu and dances on a saloon stage to the music of a little girl's crank organ. As the kid watches, a drunk from the judge's table shoots the bear, but there is nothing sacred or holy in this hunt. The prey is killed without even the intention of power or ritual and its death is a meaningless spectacle: "The bear had been shot through the midsection. He let out a low moan and he began to dance faster, dancing in silence save for the slap of his great footpads on the planks. . . . The man with the pistol fired again . . . and the bear groaned and began to reel drunkenly. He was holding his chest . . . and he began to totter and to cry like a child and he took a few last steps, dancing, and crashed to the boards" (326). This scene is the antithesis of the one that occurred in the mountains. The bear, like the last few buffalo and the defeated remnants of the native tribes, is now the hostage. In the place of the Delaware with his arm around the neck of the mighty beast who will carry him off crouches the sobbing child with her arms around the neck of the dead bear that "in its crinoline lay like some monster slain in the commission of unnatural acts" (327). This scene is capped with perhaps the most unnatural act of all: the judge's subsequent murder of the little girl, who, like most of the other children in the novel, is betrayed by the sacred hunter who should be her protector and is taken by him as prey.

The destruction and reordering of the original myth is now complete. This point for McCarthy is a meridian and a nadir, the final mastery of man over the wilderness and the prophetic embarkation of his descent. The judge tells the scalphunters, "in the affairs of man there is no waning and the noon of his expression signals the onset of night. His spirit is exhausted at the peak of his achievement. His meridian is at once his darkening and the evening of his day" (147). There is the implication here of something inevitable and preordained, more than the random tragedy of history. As the quote regarding the 300,000-year-old skull from Africa suggests, neither scalping nor any other vicious perversion is new or unique. The scalphunters and the Indians, the dancers in the saloon, the lone buffalo hunter on the empty prairie, and the long-dead scalper of the unfortunate Ethiopian whose skull now speaks to modern anthropologists are all tabernacled in the others' books (141), "each pass[ing] back the way the other had come, pursuing as all travelers must inversions without end upon other men's journeys" (121) in an "endless complexity of being and witness" (141).

The suggestion is that the myth has always contained within itself the anti-myth, the dark shadow double awaiting a Kurtz or a Holden to strip bare the original and turn it inside out. McCarthy's earth in *Blood Meridian* and many other works is hollow, full of empty caves and echoing caverns, at once womb and tomb, signifying the hollowness at the heart of all myths. There is no center to the sacred hunter myth, any more than there is to its antithesis. And yet the power of myth to move and shape us remains, and through *Blood Meridian,* McCarthy has done more than simply invert the sacred hunter and the eucharist of the wilderness; he has altered their form in several significant ways.

The most basic relationship enshrined in that myth, between man and nature, is ultimately replaced with a new ordering based upon the relationship between man and man in the form of sacred war. The death of a bear or deer, the sacrificial shedding of the blood of some symbol of divine nature, once an essential part of the ritual upon which the sacred hunter myth rested, is no longer sufficient for regeneration. Regeneration depends upon ritual, but as the judge explains, "A ritual includes the letting of blood. Rituals which fail in this requirement are but mock rituals" (329). The myth of science, therefore, is not enough. It must be enacted through the more ancient ritual of war. Because all generations following this one have been euchred of the patrimony of nature, invalidating the blood of bears or deer as sources of regeneration, the prey must now become humanity itself. The new version of the myth demands human blood, for now no other will suffice, and, therefore, as the judge suggests, the holiest of all acts is war.

And again the suggestion is that of inevitable procession toward this end. "War was always here," the judge says. "Before man was, war waited for him. The ultimate trade awaiting its ultimate practitioner" (248). War, in fact, is god, according to the judge, because, as myth or game enhanced "to its ultimate state" (249), it is the perfect embodiment of human will, the force of will made divine, driven to test itself against the very stuff of creation, "a forcing of the unity of existence" (249), beyond what the judge considers the petty concerns of moral judgments. In engaging in the act of war, in forcing the hand of existence to choose who shall live and who shall die, the sacred hunter becomes one with the prey, and man assumes the cloak of divine power himself. Moral law, good and evil, are simply trivialities enshrined by one church or another. Questions of right and wrong are subsumed by the force of human will made manifest in this mythic vision of war. To prove this notion the judge challenges Tobin, the de facto representative of religion and moral order:

> The judge searched out the circle for disputants. But what says the priest? he said.
>
> Tobin looked up. The priest does not say.
>
> The priest does not say, said the judge. . . . But the priest has said. For the priest has put by the robes of his craft and taken up the tools of that higher calling which all men honor. The priest also would be no godserver but a god himself. . . .

> I'll not secondsay you in your notions, said Tobin. Dont ask it.
>
> Ah Priest, said the judge. What could I ask of you that you've not already given? (250–51)

The judge's new myth has long ago swallowed up Tobin and the religion and morality he symbolizes, the impotent state of those institutions marked by Tobin's status as "ex" priest. The churches are empty shells, like the Anasazi village, crumbling ruins of an order dead and vanished, now "wondered at by tribes of savages" doomed to erect new churches, new edifices of stone in their attempts to "alter the structure of the universe" (146). But all such attempts, the judge insinuates, will ultimately fail. "This you see here, these ruins . . . do you not think that this will be again? Aye. And again. With other people, with other sons" (147). The judge has proven that the only thing that can truly alter creation is the brute force of human will, sharpened and focused through the lens of a mythic structure unconcerned with morality and bent to the task of godlike war. The eucharist of the wilderness has now become a eucharist of humanity.

Everyone now is a participant in the dance of war, either as hunter or as prey. All in the gang have been baptized into the new myth, have partaken in its ceremonies of cannibalism and rape. Only the kid finally attempts to renounce the dance and to assert a will independent of the judge and his anti-myth. By giving up his position as a hunter of men within this new myth, he makes himself prey. At the ruins, the judge supplied the blueprint for raising hunters, explaining that at a young age children should be put into pits with wild dogs, forced to fight lions and run naked through the desert. Only those with the most perfect and powerful wills would survive such tests (mercy, we are to assume, would produce weakness instead of strength), and, ironically of course, only those adults with the most potent of wills could administer the trials without succumbing to the urge to help the children.

The kid faces several such trials throughout the narrative and fails them. He alone of the gang answers David Brown's call for aid in removing an arrow from his leg (162). By the rules of the anti-myth, Brown should have been left on his own, like the child in the pit of wild dogs, to triumph by the force of his will alone or to fail and die in the desert. Tobin warns the kid of the danger of his actions: "Fool, he said. God will not love ye forever. . . . Dont you know he'd of took you with him? He'd of took you boy. Like a bride to the altar" (162–63).

The "he" here refers to the judge, who has earlier refused to help Brown and who tests the kid later by calling for help himself in the killing of a horse (219).

None of the other members of the gang answers him, and Tobin again warns the kid not to respond. In doing so, the kid violates the internal order of the myth, though the prospect of being taken "like a bride to the altar" by the judge is perhaps not such an appealing one. While the phrase echoes the rhetoric of the sacred marriage common to both Christianity and the sacred hunter myth and perverted by the act of rape in this new order, in this instance we can understand Tobin to intend a positive meaning. While the relationship between the judge and the kid might be more properly characterized as that between father and son rather than husband and bride, the implication at least is of renewal and rebirth, the promise of regeneration that the kid betrays.

As Tobin and the kid crouch in the desert after the slaughter at the ferry crossing, the kid receives his final chance to seize his place as hunter within the new myth and fails once again when he refuses to shoot the unarmed judge. To do so would only have been right and proper within the relationship of hunter and prey, human will against human will in sacred war, as well as within the relationship of father and son, since as the judge has said at the Anasazi ruins, it is the death of the father to which the son is entitled. When the kid will neither shoot him nor join him, the judge charges, "There's a flawed place in the fabric of your heart. . . . You alone were mutinous. You alone reserved in your soul some corner of clemency" (299).

The kid ignores the judge's warning and over the final section of the book covering the last decades of his life, attempts to return to the previous mythic order, to reestablish the relationship of the sacred hunter as guardian and protector of his community. He becomes a guide for other travelers passing through the wilderness, protecting them from the forces of nature, from Indians, and from those like his old companions who have become hunters of men. Most significantly, he begins to carry a Bible, a book already made defunct by the judge as a false book and symbol of the empty moral laws thrown down before the force of human wills in war. Like the church it represents, the Bible is a kind of ruin here, silent and without reference in the world shaped by the new myth. Especially for the illiterate kid, the Bible is a mute emblem of a fallen system, "no word of which he could read" (312).

Its futility as a symbol within the world shaped by the new order is reified by the kid's encounter with the penitents he finds butchered in a canyon and his attempts to speak with one of them:

> The kid rose and looked about at this desolate scene and then he saw alone and upright in a small niche in the rocks an old woman kneeling in a faded rebozo with her eyes cast down.

> He made his way among the corpses and stood before her. . . . She did not look up. . . . He spoke to her in a low voice. He told her that he was an American and that he was a long way from the country of his birth and that he had no family and that he had traveled much and seen many things and had been at war and endured hardships. He told her that he would convey her to a safe place, some party of her country-people who would welcome her and that she should join them for he could not leave her in this place or she would surely die.
>
> He knelt on one knee, resting the rifle before him like a staff. Abuelita, he said. No puedes escucharme?
>
> He reached into the alcove and touched her arm. . . . She weighed nothing. She was just a dried shell and she had been dead in that place for years. (315)

The kid attempts here to perform the act of confession, a ritual based upon the acknowledgement of a moral order the speaker has in some way violated, but the kid has himself been a participant, as his confession makes clear, in the destruction of that moral order that has rendered this ceremony empty and meaningless, the authority of the church now "just a dried shell." The kid has turned his back on the new myth he helped bring into being, but it is too late to revive the old ones. He prostrates himself before a dead body that cannot hear his confession and can therefore offer no absolution or forgiveness, cannot even move to accept his proffered aide, and is as mute as the Bible he carries but cannot read. He even clasps his rifle, not like a weapon of divine war, worthy of the name the judge has bestowed on his gun, the tool of death in the garden, but like a staff, symbol of the doomed priest, administrator of an empty office, and a figure the kid is said to have come to resemble.

The kid has in fact betrayed the sacred office he once occupied as a hunter of men in this new myth, and it is this betrayal for which the judge castigates him in the prison. "You came forward, he said, to take part in a work. But you were a witness against yourself. You sat in judgment on your own deeds. You put your own allowances before the judgments of history and you broke with the body of which you were pledged a part" (307). And it is for this betrayal that the judge, described as immense and bearlike (having subsumed the figures of the old myths within himself), finally kills the kid in a horrible embrace, a corrupted hug, a perversion of the act of reproduction performed in the midst of human excrement (333), and yet despite all this, an act that is holy and proper within the structure of the new myth, for after the killing the judge emerges renewed and rejuvenated to join the dance in the saloon.

If we accept Slotkin's claim that any fundamental alteration of the narrative structure of the myth signals some profound shift in the culture that produces it, then the sense of momentous change is inescapable. Here is the bloody tie binding America's mythic past to its troubled present, here in this mythic dance is the violent birth of a National Symbolic that has made heroes out of scalphunters and Indian killers and constructed the near-extinction of the buffalo and massive deforestation as symbols of triumph and mastery, the proud heritage of the modern American citizen. This is one possible interpretation of the novel's rather obscure epilogue. The man progressing over the silent plain digging postholes is striking out of the rock with his steel, the fire, and symbolically the life, "which God has put there" (337), the first step before stringing barbed wire along that "track of holes that runs to the rim of the visible ground" (337).

The barbed wire fence is a potent and deeply paradoxical symbol in the American West. On one hand, it is the triumphant emblem of Anglo America's conquest of the land once referred to as the Great American Desert, of the sheer force of human will necessary to empty it of those animals like the buffalo that do not serve Anglo America's needs and to fill it instead with cattle—nature tamed and controlled by the sharp-edged product of Eastern factories. It is also, for many Westerners, the sign of some final closure, usually expressed nostalgically as the loss of the wandering horseman's right to travel freely and without restriction across the landscape. That wandering horseman, the lone cowboy with his bedroll and his rifle, is the most commonly recognized modern American expression of the sacred hunter, the lone male in the wilderness, here digging the postholes that mark his own demise and performing the final fencing-in of the natural world.

The plain in the epilogue is empty of life, no buffalo, no bears, wolves, or antelope, the patrimony of nature gone, only "bones and the gatherers of bones" (337), following behind the diminished hunter striking out hole after hole. The act of the posthole digger "seems less the pursuit of some continuance than the verification of a principle, a validation of sequence and causality" (337), the consequence of our national acceptance of the judge's perverted anti-myth, of the disruption of the continuum identified by Dana Phillips in which some balance or relationship between man and nature has been destroyed and replaced with a mythic structure few besides McCarthy have dared to gaze at unflinchingly. American identity, as constructed through the national(ist) narrative of frontier myth, cannot be seen as innocent, either of intent or deed. Nor can national identity as the product of myth be viewed as essential in any way. Rather, identity must be seen as fragile, tenuous, and unfixed, as McCarthy suggests all empires of man are. In the first of his Western works, McCarthy has recast the lens of myth through which American history and identity is viewed, thus challenging the mythic language by which the American nation understands itself, its beliefs, and its role in the world.

CHAPTER 2

"Pledged in Blood"

Truth and Redemption in Cormac McCarthy's *All the Pretty Horses*

> *Even when the romanticizing of the past, as well as the present cultural identity, is exposed as a self-serving illusion . . . the mythic element that permeates the popular consciousness may not easily be exorcised as useless trivia since it has come to assume a life of its own in the group's imagination.*
>
> GENARO PADILLA

As many critics have noted, it is no coincidence that the action of *All the Pretty Horses* takes place exactly one hundred years after that of *Blood Meridian.* In many ways, *Pretty Horses* is the offspring of that book, an elegy for a romanticized way of life, a code of honor, a mythical world both birthed and brutally murdered in *Blood Meridian.* In *Pretty Horses,* we see the modern embodiment of the ancient myth of the sacred hunter—the sacred cowboy. The figure of the hunter engaged in holy communion with nature has, by the end of *Blood Meridian,* been replaced with that of the cowboy digging postholes, preparing to string barbed wire across the tamed body of the wilderness so that he may populate with cattle that which he so mercilessly emptied of buffalo. The figure of the cowboy personifies America's most cherished myths, combining ideas of American exceptionalism, Manifest Destiny, rugged individualism, frontier democracy, communion with and conquest of the natural world, and the righteous triumph of the white race. In *All the Pretty Horses,* McCarthy brutally deconstructs the fantasy narratives needed to uphold these mythic icons.

The figure of the sacred cowboy is one of our most potent National Fantasies, visible in everything from ads for blue jeans to car commercials to popular films. I will argue, however, that this mythic figure, like that of the hunter that preceded it, is bound to crumble, for it is hollow at its core and stripped bare by McCarthy in *All the Pretty Horses*. As John Grady Cole slowly begins to recognize the fragility and falseness of his life, he seeks a return to the imagined innocence of the sacred cowboy of the mythic past, only to discover no such return is possible.

John Grady's quest signifies the gap in the National Symbolic the fantasy of the cowboy on the open range has been unable to cover. Unlike the random trajectory of *Blood Meridian*'s kid, however, John Grady's quest is made poignant for American readers by the fact that the imagined version of the cowboy code of conduct so wholeheartedly and unquestioningly accepted by John Grady at the start of the novel is at once admirable and utterly untenable, full of contradiction and hypocrisy. As American readers, we cannot help but respond to the evocation of that myth through such a sympathetic and likeable character. This is, perhaps, one reason *All the Pretty Horses* has so often been labeled McCarthy's most "accessible" work of fiction and is his first novel to appear on the *New York Times* bestseller list. Indeed, Vereen Bell notes it is probable that "this novel has already sold more copies than all of McCarthy's previous novels combined" ("Between the Wish," 927).

The life John Grady has been living on his family's Texas ranch is a romantic fantasy, familiar to every American through innumerable novels, films, grade-school history texts, beer commercials, and cigarette advertisements. It is nonetheless a mask, a rose-colored cliché of the National Symbolic barely hiding the falseness at its core. That this particular myth strides about on feet of clay is made apparent, not just through the immanent sale of the ranch, but through the persistent return of all that this version of National Fantasy attempts to deny and repress: the truth of its conception so brutally revealed in *Blood Meridian*. As I noted in the introduction, belief in this mythic narrative and the innocent vision it presents of America, American history, and American identity requires fierce and careful denial of both the imperial theft of land that allowed for Anglo settlement and the inherent racism and classism necessary to maintain and justify the social order born of that history. Through the all-American character of John Grady, with his innocence and romanticism coupled with stubborn, self-serving blindness, McCarthy lovingly evokes that myth and at the same time strips away the layers of fantasy that make belief in it possible.

The violent past thrusts itself into the present in *Pretty Horses* almost immediately, as the novel opens with John Grady leaving the funeral of his cowboy-rancher grandfather to ride "the western fork of the old Comanche road coming down out of the Kiowa country. . . . the ancient road was shaped before him in the rose and canted light like a dream of the past where the painted ponies and the riders of that lost nation came down out of the north . . . all of them pledged in blood and redeemable in blood only. . . . nation and ghost of nation passing in a soft chorale across that mineral waste to darkness bearing lost to all history and all remembrance like a grail the sum of their secular and transitory and violent lives" (5). The very people scalped for profit in *Blood Meridian* to allow for white settlement, the nation made ghost so that generations of Grady's and Cole's could run cattle, limn with darkness and blood the wholesome myth of that most privileged of Western icons—the independent rancher. The vanished Comanche traverse the gap in the National Symbolic left bare by this version of National Fantasy that resolutely ignores the reality, the non-innocence, of its own history. They are "pledged in blood and redeemable in blood only," but so is the nation that replaced them and that rides the same trail, side by side with their ghosts. John Grady, in his innocent acceptance of the non-innocent myth of the sacred cowboy, realizes only faintly this debt of blood and not at all that it will fall on him to pay if he wishes to redeem himself from the hollowness, falsity, and self-deception (sweetly romantic though it may be) of that myth.

This metaphorical joining of one ghostly dream to another is established again through the image of the vanished, and now safely romanticized, Comanches. John Grady's father, another dying cowboy-rancher, tells him, "We're like the Comanches was two hundred years ago" (25) in an attempt to soften the impending loss of their ranch, to evoke the presence of one "dream of the past" to join in mourning the passing of another, equally "secular and transitory and violent." But it is yet another artifact of the past, which comes to John Grady as he sits at his dead grandfather's desk, that best signifies not only the persistent return of history through the liminal spaces of myth but also the lesson that John Grady must finally learn about the deceptive nature of the world seen through the blinders of National Fantasy. As he sits in the darkened office, he can see through the window "The black crosses of the old telegraph poles yoked across the constellations passing east to west. His grandfather said the Comanche would cut the wires and splice them back with horsehair" (11). In the illusion created by the splicing of the severed wires, McCarthy demonstrates the difficulty of seeing the world, not as one would wish it to be, but as it actually is. While the wires may appear whole, they are nonetheless not functional. To paraphrase the Dueña Alfonsa, this is the difference between that which is true and that which it is merely useful to believe, between the dream and the reality, between myth and history. This is the world that lies waiting between the wish and the thing.

It is John Grady's naive and romantic inability to distinguish the truth, which the Dueña Alfonsa explains to be not "what is righteous but merely what is so" (240), that both moves her to pay his and Rawlin's way out of prison and ultimately to reject his suit for Alejandra's hand. As she tells John Grady before she begins her tale, "You will see that those things which disposed me in your favor were the very things which led me to decide against you in the end" (231). Her entire monologue, the history of her life, is told for John Grady's benefit, and indeed, John Grady is a sort of male version of her young and idealistic self. Her journey may be seen as a tightly compressed parable of his.

As their stories start, both are seventeen years old, romantic, idealistic, enamored of an imagined code of justice and honor in a world built upon injustice and corruption. Both are believers in a nostalgic myth, a form of National Fantasy that shows them, as Alfonsa puts it, "how the world must become if I were to live in it" (233), and that therefore does not allow them to see the world as it really is. The danger of such deliberate, albeit romantic, blindness is illustrated by the fates of Gustavo and Francisco, Alfonsa's fellow idealists tortured and shot by mobs directed by the corrupt General Huerta while the ambassador at the American embassy saves President Taft the embarrassment of having to explain why the United States does not intercede by deliberately neglecting to forward to Washington the frantic telegram delivered into his hands.[1]

Despite the way in which many have read the novel, this is not a matter of juxtaposing innocent American romanticism with the brutal, violent realities of an inherently corrupt Mexico.[2] American culpability in Mexican history and politics is clearly established in *Blood Meridian* and openly alluded to in *Pretty Horses*, especially in Alfonsa's narrative. Nor, I believe, is McCarthy attempting to posit America as the site of modernity and Mexico as simply a dream of the romanticized past, as Vereen Bell suggests, although John Grady may initially see it in just that way. Bell writes in "Between the Wish and the Thing the World Lies Waiting" that "John Grady and Rawlins escape for a time the dissociating effects of the technology and capital of the new American order, but what they get from their adopted ancient culture is an attractive but totalitarian hierarchy—the autocratic rule of families, at best, and at worst, of brute power instead of law. In Enlightenment terms, a dignified ancient culture is also, inescapably, a primitive one" (926). McCarthy has gone to great lengths, however, to point out that Mexican culture is no more "ancient" or "primitive" than American culture. Do the roots of Mexican culture stretch back to pre-Columbian indigenous peoples? John Grady rides through the ghosts of just such peoples on his own ranch and is watched by their living descendants upon his return to Texas. Is Mexico ruled by "brute power instead of law"? The Coles run their cattle on land stolen from native peoples by "brute power instead of law." Is John Grady a nomad without a home in Mexico? He's still a homeless wanderer when he re-crosses the border and the brute power of law itself, explained to him by his father's attorney, has still robbed him of the patrimony his ancestors stole from the Comanches. He is as helpless before its implacable and pitiless advance as he is before the corrupt captain in the Mexican jail. Neither can be cajoled, neither can be reasoned with, neither shows mercy or the slightest acknowledgment of John Grady's wishes, his code of honor, his view of how the world should be rather than how the world is.

In other words, the myth of the sacred cowboy that demands that a worthy young man should end up with a ranch of his own, a lovely young wife, and "all the pretty horses" in a gloriously guilt-free Eden simply by virtue of being Anglo, male, and the descendent of colonizers, functions in neither world, and this is McCarthy's point. If we fall into the trap of believing that the code of the sacred cowboy was valid at some romanticized time in America's past, we will naturally assume that in an equally romanticized "old Mexico," where John Grady has symbolically traveled back in time, it will once again function properly. The world will be as the myth says it is.

Reality, of course, proves the world to be far different. It is possible to speculate that had John Grady been Señor Rocha's son, rather than an American adventurer come to deflower his teenage daughter, the myth would still appear to function, although McCarthy would not have much of a story. John Grady would inherit La Purísima and all would be right with the world, at least for John Grady if not for the Indians whose land he would possess. But I believe Alfonsa's warning to be equally valid for the Rochas as for John Grady. While the myth may be crumbling under its own weight of blood in the United States a few decades sooner, time and history move in Mexico as well as north of the border. The signs of change (Señora Rocha's continued absence in the city, like John Grady's mother; Señor Rocha's travel via private plane) all indicate the relentless advance of history, technology, and capitalism. As Bell acknowledges, there is no escape possible, because "There is no human place outside of time, and where human places are there are also the constructs and institutional artifacts of history" (926).

This is as true, however, for the United States as it is for Mexico. It is not some ancient or primitive quality in Mexico that defeats John Grady; it is the hollowness and blindness of his faith, or more properly, the hollowness and non-innocence of that myth upon which he has chosen to place his faith.[3] Like the peasants in Alfonsa's tale who desperately attempt to sell objects no one wants, John Grady clings to the values of a myth that hides the true nature of the world. He refuses or is unable to recognize that the falseness of the sacred cowboy is equivalent to the broken bits of machinery the peasants gather from the roads. The peasants' faith in a myth, in this case the value of all things associated with the industrialized world coupled with a profound ignorance of the true nature of that world, both strengthens them and dooms them. The courage to see the world without ignorance and without faith, essentially without sentiments, however attractive they may be, is what the Dueña Alfonsa attempts to teach John Grady to find through the story of her own life and the march of history in Mexico.

The United States and Mexico are not opposite ends of some nostalgic timeline here. They are, in fact, more properly twinned versions of each other. What John Grady and Rawlins find restored to them in Mexico is simply a magnification of what they left behind in Texas—cowboys and charros, ponies and grullos, ranch house and hacienda. Yes, there is a social hierarchy in Mexico, but the Mexicans dealing with John Grady and Rawlins are simply more honest than the Americans in acknowledging the class differences that molded the lives of the two boys from the start. Back in Texas, it is Rawlins whose family lives as virtual squatters in a ramshackled house and John Grady whose family owns an eighteen-thousand-acre ranch. And in Mexico, it is Rawlins who eats in the bunkhouse with the rest of the ranch hands, while John Grady takes his meals privately in the kitchen of the hacienda, waited on by La Purísima's servants. In fact, those breakfast scenes at La Purísima are nearly identical to the ones that take place in John Grady's ranch house in Texas, right down to the paired Mexican women cooking and serving him his food. When the padrón of the prison asks John Grady if he learned to speak Spanish from servants, he maintains, "We didn't have no servants. We had people worked on the place" (191). There is, of course, no practical difference between the two. John Grady is attempting to uphold another facet of the sacred cowboy myth as it has been used to construct the National Symbolic, the fantasy that class hierarchies do not exist in America in general, but most especially not in the American West where a somehow truer and purer form of American democracy is supposed to have eliminated such corrupt, Old World cultural manifestations.

At the heart of this myth is the sacred cowboy who, as a modern expression of the sacred hunter, is descended from what Annette Kolodny defines as the American Pastoral. Although she traces the figure of the yeoman farmer as the hero of this literature, I would argue that the hunter-cowboy figure holds far more sway in the American imagination and the National Symbolic simply by virtue of its romantic and mythic air. Nonetheless, both figures have much in common. Along with the idea that both possess a special connection to the natural landscape is the fantasy that they created in the "New World" a classless and egalitarian society. Kolodny argues that the diction of much American literature of the nineteenth and twentieth centuries has "had a tendency to level all social elements to an Arcadian democracy" deliberately appealing to "that quality of fraternal and communal democracy that has always been an element of pastoral" (52).

Part of what drove the evolution of the sacred hunter into the figure of the sacred cowboy was the very success of American imperialism's virtual genocide of Native Americans. As Slotkin notes, with the official government closing of the last geographic frontier in the United States in 1891 and the final confinement of Native Americans on reservations, the savage racial war at the heart of the frontier myth needed a new narrative form, a new frontier, and a new set of savages against which to pit white civilization. The savage war soon shifted onto the international stage, providing mythic justification for American imperialism abroad as brave Anglo boys fought to civilize the dark-skinned savages of the Philippines, Cuba, China, and other countries. The myth also adjusted to changing situations at home, morphing from a source of democracy to a source of empire, from that which produced a race of egalitarian heroes to that which justified a class of racially privileged managers. For the United States, as for Great Britain, the real business of empire has always been business. Slotkin argues that when the myth of the savage war came to be applied to social classes, it pitted civilized white owners and managers against savage, often dark-skinned or foreign, workers. Like the savage Apaches and Comanches, the savage masses of poor workers had to be brought under the control of white civilization and those wealthy, elite males who imagined themselves its spokesmen. Through the nineteenth and twentieth centuries, small farms increasingly became agribusinesses, mom-and-pop manufacturing concerns became multinational corporate giants, and family ranches became part of the massive Cattle Growers Association or, in a final irony, like the Grady-Cole spread were sold to oil companies or other industries.

Even U.S. foreign policy and American attitudes towards the rest of the world are shaped and directed by this mythic vision. It is no coincidence, for example, that support for Israel is stronger in the United States than in any other country in the world and within the United States itself is strongest among white Southerners and weakest among African Americans. When white Americans, especially those from the South, look at the Middle East through the racialized lens of this privileging myth, they see a relatively small number of "civilized" middle-class Israelis struggling to control masses of poor "savage" Palestinians who, like poor blacks and other minorities in the United States, represent both a major source of cheap labor and the potential for violent resistance. In the Middle East, of course, one could argue that this potential, mirroring the longest-standing nightmare of the white American South, has been realized with the terror of suicide bombings and intifadas. For many white Americans, whose identities and values have been defined and directed by the myth of the sacred cowboy and his savage war against the heathen, no course but whole-hearted, unquestioning support of Israel is imaginable. Any other response would necessitate a challenge to the most essentialized and stubbornly unexamined aspects of American culture, history, race relations, and social structure, calling into question the rhetoric about democracy and classless, color-blind egalitarianism that must work to maintain this myth.

This, however, is exactly what McCarthy challenges in *All the Pretty Horses.* Far from contrasting an imagined American egalitarianism with a Mexican caste system, for McCarthy Mexico merely illuminates the hypocrisy of the American myth. John Grady lacks money when he reaches La Purísima, and that is doubtless Alejandra's father's main objection to him, because the padrón recognizes immediately that while John Grady and Rawlins may have equally empty pockets, they are not social equals or members of the same class, even back in Texas. The padrón becomes a sort of foster father to John Grady, while he is never more than an employer to Rawlins. John Grady acknowledges this during his confession to the Texas judge when he admits that he betrayed Señor Rocha by sleeping with his daughter, admitting his guilt for violating the unspoken rules regarding behavior towards women of one's own social class. He expresses no sense of guilt whatsoever over his later visits to the whorehouses of Juarez. The girls there with whom he has sex are also, of course, someone's daughters, but conspicuously not daughters inhabiting the same privileged place in the social hierarchy as Alejandra and John Grady.

In this way, Alejandra and John Grady are also more like twinned images than diametrically opposed opposites. Like the young Alfonsa, they both still see the world as they wish it to be, from the privileged position of their social class, cocooned in the fragile paradise of their respective ranches where the descendants of the peoples their ancestors conquered and whose land they stole are now servants and outcasts. Alejandra and John Grady are shielded, at least initially, from having to face the world without their myths, clinging like the peasants from the countryside to bolts and "wornout part[s] of a machine that no one could even know the use of" (231). Like the young Alfonsa, neither of them can see that what may appear innocent, right, *whole,* is, like the spliced telegraph wire, unsound and nonfunctional, merely an illusion of the real. Alejandra, in the end, sees the futility of refusing to select "between the dream and the reality," which is, unfair though it may be, that by losing his family's ranch John Grady has also lost his claim to membership in the privileged managerial class. The knowledge that follows this epiphany marks her with the sadness John Grady sees at their final meeting, just as Alfonsa tells him she is marked through the loss of her fingers and as John Grady will mark himself with the red-hot barrel of his own pistol.

There is some disagreement among scholars as to what, if any, lesson John Grady (and presumably McCarthy's reader) learns after his adventures in Mexico and his discourses with the Dueña Alfonsa. Tom Pilkington claims the realization that "the individual is alone in a cold, indifferent universe—appears to be the sum of John Grady's experiences in the novel" (314). Vereen Bell asserts that the point of the novel is "whether John Grady can endure such gratuitous tribulation with his hardheaded boy's idealism intact" (921), while Diane Luce in "When You Wake" disagrees with Bell and argues that, on the contrary, John Grady's "idealism misleads him sometimes so seriously as to compromise his integrity. I think the point of the novel is more whether John Grady can understand and accept the consequences of his own choices . . . without abandoning himself and thus breaking faith with others" (165). What John Grady must abandon, however, is not his idealism per se but rather his blind faith in a mythic construct that hides from him the true nature of the world and therefore also the knowledge of his proper place within it.

The second half of this equation, which Luce identifies as not "breaking faith with others," is even more difficult to attain than the simple recognition that we are alone in a world that is not always what it appears to be. The Dueña Alfonsa has come to terms with the nature of the world as she sees it. It is, as Gustavo told her, "that those who have endured some misfortune will always be set apart but that it is just that misfortune which is their gift and which is their strength and that they must make their way back into the common enterprise of man for without they do so it cannot go forward and they themselves will wither in bitterness" (235). Alfonsa continues her discourse with John Grady, saying, "Long before morning I knew that what I was seeking to discover was a thing I'd always known. That all courage was a form of constancy. That it was always himself that the coward abandoned first" (235). And yet we know that the price Gustavo paid for rejoining "the common enterprise of man" is violent death at the hands of a mob he had sacrificed his fortune to aid. Gustavo, in effect, reached out for the world again with both hands. Alfonsa, however, seems to have achieved an almost zen-like equilibrium. She grasps the world with one hand and disengages from it with the other, never allowing herself to be pulled either into paralyzing bitterness or blind idealism. This is the constancy she identifies as courage. She tells John Grady, "You spoke of my disappointments. If such they are they have only made me reckless. My grandniece is the only future I contemplate and where she is concerned I can only put all my chips forward. . . . I know what she cannot. That there is nothing to lose. I don't know what sort of world she will live in and I have no fixed opinions concerning how she should live in it. I only know that if she does not come to value what is true above what is useful it will make little difference whether she lives at all" (239–40). Alfonsa sees through the facade of the various myths constructing her world, that of Mexicans "mad for society" (230), of the Spanish who believe in nothing unless it be made to bleed, of the romantic and idealistic notions of social justice she embraced in Europe. But unlike John Grady's father, who, having seen the world "right at last . . . as it had always been" (23), is destroyed by the sight, Alfonsa is moved to action, strengthened rather than weakened by the knowledge that "there is nothing to lose" or perhaps more properly that what one loses is the sentimental blinders of myth. She releases her hold on any belief about what the future should look like but holds on to the reality of its existence firmly through her love for Alejandra.

John Grady struggles down the hard road to reach such a place himself through the final section of the novel. He begins to realize the hollowness of the myths into which he has poured his faith even before his long dialogue with Alfonsa, as he lies in the prison after the knife fight and feels a child's sorrow welling up inside him "but it brought with it such pain that he stopped it cold and began at once his new life and the living of it breath to breath" (203). But while his new life, seen without the rosy filter of the mythic fantasy through which he has always viewed the world, might be said to begin here, his own place within that world is still unclear. No new mythic structure has emerged to replace the old one, and this is perhaps the most important part of the Dueña Alfonsa's lesson for John Grady: that to distinguish what is true from what is useful to believe means to discard all the myths one's culture holds dear and make one's way in the world alone, with nothing but one's own courage to call upon, and all without ever falling into hopeless bitterness. This sort of existentialist epiphany, however, will never leave one unmarked or even entirely whole. Like Gustavo with his glass eye, and the Dueña with her missing fingers, such knowledge exacts a price, leaving one arguably reduced.

John Grady's task then is to come to terms with this loss, signified for him by the loss of Alejandra and to the rest of the world (represented by the Texas judge to whom he confesses) by the pistol-burned scars on his leg. He must somehow achieve the balance that will allow him to rejoin the common enterprise of man and determine his place within a world now completely altered and yet totally unchanged. John Grady's first step in this process occurs when he tells his and Rawlins's story to the children outside of Torreón. Just as the Dueña Alfonsa's story was a sort of compressed parable of John Grady's, here John Grady is reifying, reducing, and compressing his own story for the children. "He told them how they had come from another country, two young horsemen riding their horses, and they had met with a third who had no money nor food to eat nor scarcely clothes to cover himself and that he had come to ride with them and share with them in all they had" (243–44). The story is presented as a parable distilled down to its mythic parts, and its inherent recognition of the role of myth in shaping the world reflects John Grady's internalization of at least part of the Dueña Alfonsa's lesson.[4]

It is also apparent that he cannot entirely let go of the magical and innocent vision of the world as it is constructed through the myth of the sacred cowboy. There is romance and adventure in the image of "two young horsemen," and within that mythic structure and under that sanitized code, what is right is more important than what is so. What is so is that John Grady is riding the horse given to him by the Dueña Alfonsa. What is right is that he recover his own horse, no matter how foolish or blindly romantic his attempt to do so may be. The fact that he does recover his and Rawlins's horses, and Blevins's as well, *feels* right to generations of American readers raised on Zane Gray and *Gunsmoke* and immersed in the parameters of a National Symbolic constructed by such fantasies, even while we recognize the stupidity behind it.[5]

John Grady is, upon his return to Texas, caught between two visions of the world, unable to return to the safe confines of the mythic past and as yet equally incapable of seeing how he must live his life in the future. He exists in a liminal space beyond myth but not yet within history, a space within which "he felt wholly alien to the world although he loved it still" (282). His unfixed liminal status, betwixt and between myth and reality, truth and history, Mexico and the United States, is figured by his physical appearance, like "some apparition out of the vanished past" (287) with his horses, guns, and

Mexican serape and his inability to properly assess his relationship to his world to the point that he must ask what day it is and is surprised to discover it is Thanksgiving. His quest to return Blevins's horse to its rightful owner is more properly a quest to release himself from the last hold of the myth of the sacred cowboy, signified in the National Symbolic by the image of the horse. His confession to the Texas judge does nothing to alleviate his pain since what he receives from the judge is essentially the same lesson given to him by the Dueña Alfonsa: the task of fixing a way for himself in the world is one he must accomplish alone.

As if to reify for him the empty and dead status of the sacred cowboy myth and the impossibility of the innocent return to a non-innocent past, the last two sights John Grady sees within the narrative are the living descendants of the ghost nation of the Comanches, camped in their wickiups among the pumps of the Yates oil field and a solitary bull in the empty and lifeless desert "rolling in the dust against the bloodred sunset like an animal in sacrificial torment" (302). There is no neat and happy ending here. John Grady "passed and paled into the darkening land, the world to come" (302), but whether he has found the epistemology that will enable him to live within that world or if he will simply vanish into it is not clear.

One may well ask at this point, given the rather simple trajectory of the plot, what lifts this story above the level of dime novel Western or simple coming-of-age tale. Oddly, or perhaps appropriately, the answer seems to revolve in part around horses. Vereen Bell notes that "the deepest continuity with life in this novel is through horses" (922), but horses resound here with a symbolic significance that functions on a number of metaphysical, even mystical levels. Horses are inextricably linked to the mythic cowboy within the National Symbolic. More so even than the cow or the gun, the horse defines the cowboy's status as sacred, special, uniquely American. (And of course, Mexican as well, as McCarthy is certainly aware. The common Spanish term for gentleman is *caballero*—literally horseman.)

Advertisers have long realized the appeal inherent in this popular metaphorical connection, as a quick glance at any ad for Marlboro cigarettes, the best-selling brand in the United States and abroad, makes clear. And as was noted in the introduction, even America's most successful car company gave its most successful vehicles the names Pinto, Mustang, and Bronco—distinctly Western words for horses. Americans have long been trained to respond to the image of cowboys and their horses, and if the mounted cowboy signifies the will of the American people in action, taming the Wild West and conquering the wilderness, the horse symbolizes the cowboy's connection to that wilderness. And in an uneasy juxtaposition, the image of a herd of wild horses thundering across some dramatic Western landscape has become one of the primary mythic signifiers by which we refer to wild and untamed nature. The tension uniting these images is that lurking off-screen so to speak, behind the wild herd and just out of our sight, is the cowboy with his lasso, the empty corral, the waiting saddle, bridle, bit, and spur. The process of breaking the wild horse, branding it, claiming and utilizing it in the further subduing of nature through fences, cattle, and roads, follows unseen, behind the image of the wild herd. It is a complex and powerful metaphor of desire and domination, of colonialist nostalgia and Manifest Destiny. Again, Kolodny has identified this paradox as inherent in the American Pastoral. She writes that "In the course of civilizing the landscape . . . man makes of it his helpless victim and inevitably betrays an earlier or hoped-for intimacy" (46). This destruction of the dream in the act of achieving it, which Kolodny says becomes one of the major themes of American fiction, sounds a "note of nostalgia for an irrevocably lost pastoral landscape" (46). And yet that loss, she argues, impels us "both to continue pursuing the fantasy in daily life, and, when that failed, to codify it as part of the culture's shared dream life" (7).

For McCarthy, the image of the wild, free herd and the mounted cowboy in pursuit of it is a metaphor through which to explore the deceptive matrix mapping the relationship of modern Americans to their land and the difficult metaphysical problem of *being* in the world—the very question John Grady rides out of Mexico still struggling to answer. If the Dueña Alfonsa is there to teach John Grady about the dangerous blindness of myth and the necessity of recognizing the truth, horses serve to teach him the nature of that truth and how one should finally live with it.

The horse-breaking episode at the hacienda is an ironic foreshadowing of the experiences John Grady will go through later in the novel. The mozo, Luís, tells him that "the souls of horses mirror the souls of men more closely than men suppose" but that while all horses share a common soul, sadly "among men there was no such communion" (111). John Grady's first act at La Purísima is to break the communion among the wild herd, to force them to "reckon slowly with the remorselessness of this rendering of their fluid and collective selves into that condition of separate and helpless paralysis" (105). Soon they are all roped and motionless "with the voice of the breaker still running in their brains like the voice of some god come to inhabit them" (105).

The illusory communion John Grady feels with his life and his history through the comforting myth of the sacred cowboy is broken in Mexico and he is left by Alfonsa like the hobbled horses in the corral, still alive but divided and paralyzed. To regain a sense of being, of connection to the world, a sense of the proper order of things and his own place within that order, John Grady must learn to recognize the mirror of his own soul within that of horses, which for McCarthy represent what Bell terms an "invisible bond with the powers of the earth" (923). Horses represent the sacred, and for McCarthy that most often means the world of nature, or as Tom Pilkington says, "McCarthy's horses . . . represent the vital life force of the universe. They stand for what *is*, pristine and unfallen nature in its most elemental form" (319).

The world of men and the world of nature are not really separated for McCarthy, and it is the task of reconnecting those worlds that drives many of his characters. The complex forces that bind them together, which illustrate the nature of truth and life and being in the world, are revealed to John Grady through two important dreams. In the first, he is shown both the collective nature of the soul of horses, who never question their relationship with the natural world, and his own connection to it through them.

> That night he dreamt of horses in a field on a high plain where the spring rains had brought up the grass and the wildflowers out of the ground and the flowers ran all blue and yellow far as the eye could see and in the dream he was among the horses running and in the dream he himself could run with the horses and he coursed the young mares and fillies over the plain where their rich bay and their rich chestnut colors shone in the sun and the young colts ran with their dams and trampled down the flowers in a haze of pollen that hung in the sun like powdered gold and they ran he and the horses out along the high mesas where the ground resounded under their running hooves and they flowed and changed and ran and their manes and tails blew off of them like spume and there was nothing else at all in that high world and they moved all of them in a resonance that was like a music among them and they were none of them afraid horse nor colt nor mare and they ran in the resonance which is the world itself and which cannot be spoken but only praised. (161–62)

The language in this single remarkable sentence is patently spiritual, mystical, even biblical, evoking the sacred nature underlying all myths. John Grady touches the sacred in the world through the body of horses, which by the end of the dream he has become. Words and language, the providence of the divided souls of men, are inadequate here. The world cannot be spoken, and it is the attempt to do so, to construct a world though the deceptive structures of myth rather than to experience it directly, that veils the true nature of the world, drowns out the music and resonance of it, brings chaos and disorder. Pilkington implies that for McCarthy, nature itself is violent and chaotic. He compares *All the Pretty Horses* to a novel by R. G. Vliet, which takes its epigraph from a Wallace Stevens poem: "We live in an old chaos of the sun." "This is existentialism in a nutshell," Pilkington says, "since nature is chaotic, meaning and order must be forged from within the individual" (312). I would argue, however, that it is not nature that is chaotic for McCarthy; rather chaos is introduced into natural order by disordered humanity, signified in John Grady's "breaking" of the wild horses at the La Purìsima corrals in accordance with the myth of the sacred cowboy, a myth that disguises not only its own violent and disordered nature but the true nature of the world and its effect on it, as well.

The dream of the Eden of horses is paired with a second dream later in the novel, after John Grady has spoken with the Dueña Alfonsa about the importance of truth. He has already returned to La Encantada to steal back his and Rawlins's horses and has not entirely come to terms with the loss of the mythic world that had sustained him.

> In his sleep he could hear the horses stepping among the rocks and he could hear them drink from the shallow pools in the dark where the rocks lay smooth and rectilinear as the stones of ancient ruins and the water from their muzzles dripped and rang like water dripping in a well and in his sleep he dreamt of horses and the horses in his dream moved gravely among the tilted stones like horses come upon an antique site where some ordering of the world had failed and if anything had been written on the stones the weathers had taken it away again and the horses were wary and moved with great circumspection carrying in their blood as they did the recollection of this and other places where horses once had been and would be again. Finally what he saw in his dream was that the order in the horse's heart was more durable for it was written in a place where no rain could erase it. (280)

The symbolism here, with the artificial order of the human soul revealed as false and transitory, is fairly obvious, but the irony of course is how this knowledge can help John Grady, who is, after all, a man and not a horse. He may run with horses in his dreams, but when he awakens, he still must find a way to live within the world of men, chaotic and disordered as that world may be. Simply loving horses and the natural world they represent, as John Grady does from the outset, is obviously not enough, and this quest, carried on in the liminal spaces of the plot of *Pretty Horses* and within the guise of a genre commonly famed for its lack of metaphysical concerns, is what finally drives the action—not lost loves, roundups, cattle drives, or prison-yard knife fights— and it is the complexity of this search that makes the novel, despite its "accessibility," so typically McCarthyesque and so important in understanding how and why the icons and figures of the mythic West continue to wield such power in American culture today.

In *Pretty Horses* McCarthy has manipulated the most familiar forms of National Fantasy, icons that construct the most basic images commonly held in America of identity, nationality, and culture, to make the coming-of-age of John Grady a story that speaks to the coming-of-age of a nation and the sorrowful and necessary death of a National Fantasy. The ending here is ambiguous, not necessarily hopeful. As promised in the opening chapter, John Grady has redeemed himself in blood from the nostalgic blindness at the heart of the sacred cowboy myth, but whether this redemption is enough to carry him forward into the world to come remains obscured and unspoken at the close of this novel.

It becomes tragically clear, however, in his final fate in *Cities of the Plain*. It is evident from the opening scene of this third book in McCarthy's Borderlands trilogy that the mythical world of the sacred cowboy is dead and gone, scarcely viable even in the dreams of those who wish to live in it. It exists entirely in the realm of myth and imagination. In the first scene of the novel, John Grady, Billy, and several other cowboys employed on a small ranch in southeastern New Mexico sit in a whorehouse in Juarez, across the border from El Paso, calling each other "cowboy" over and over, in a sort of desperate incantation, as though trying to banish the impending seizure of the ranch by the U.S. military as part of its base at Alamagordo and their own inevitable unemployment and obsolescence. Their constant naming of themselves and their profession however is futile—the invocation of a mythic world and an identity already defunct. The opening scene of the novel is lively and humorous, full of comic verve, but the feeling is that of a B-grade Western, as if John Grady, Billy, and the others are acting out a scene at once familiar, nostalgic, but already a cliché, more fantasy than real. The heart of the ranch where they live and work, Mr. Johnson's daughter Margaret, is dead before the narrative begins, and Mr. Johnson himself is a walking ghost, slowly falling into senility, wandering off into the desert in the middle of the night dressed only in his nightshirt and having to be gently led back to his house. It is John Grady who looks after him in his increasingly common attacks of confusion, sitting up with him at the kitchen table until morning so it will appear to the others that the old man simply got up very early, though in reality all the hands on the ranch are aware of their employer's condition.

Although attempting to mask the disintegration of the old cowboy, his way of life, and his doomed ranch is a kind-hearted act, it is an early hint that John Grady has chosen to ignore the lesson the Dueña Alfonsa attempted to teach him. As with the pretty young whore he sees in Juarez whose long black hair makes her resemble Alejandra, John Grady chooses to see the world of the ranch in the way he wishes it to be, not in the way it is.

Like *All the Pretty Horses,* the plot of *Cities of the Plain* is simple and straightforward. John Grady convinces himself he is in love with the girl, Magdalena. She is killed by the pimp who manages the whorehouse as she tries to run away to marry John Grady. He and the pimp kill each other after John Grady challenges the man to a knife fight in order to revenge Magdalena's murder. John Grady, the last real cowboy, who has adhered to the cowboy code throughout the novel, dies along with the ranch and the imagined way of life they represent.

In effect however, John Grady has committed suicide, both literally and figuratively. In order to get close enough to stab the pimp, John Grady deliberately allows the man to give him a fatal wound, and in order to deny the truth he sees before him every day on the ranch, that the myth upon which he has structured his life is hollow at its core and shattering to pieces around him, he chooses time and time again to ignore what the world shows him and to cling blindly to a vision of things as he would like them to be. He is unable to move into the future without the comforting blinders of myth, as the Dueña Alfonsa has done, and unlike her, chooses death rather than truth. As the Dueña Alfonsa told him three years earlier, it is always himself the coward abandons first.

To call John Grady a coward may seem far-fetched. After all, he has exhibited great physical courage and is presented in both novels as an entirely good-intentioned and likeable character, one of the few in McCarthy's oeuvre. But the fate he chooses for himself in *Cities of the Plain* succinctly answers the question left hanging at the close of *All the Pretty Horses,* where John Grady disappears ambiguously "into the world to come" (302).

The myth of the sacred cowboy and the structures of the National Symbolic it supports are, in the end, an epistemology of death, dashing and romantic without doubt, but hollow, false, blood-stained, and too frightened of the truth to see the world as it is or to live in the one to come. Through the tragic figure of John Grady and the choices he makes, which lead inevitably to death, McCarthy challenges his readers to look clearly upon the consequences to American culture and the rest of the world of our acceptance of the figure of the sacred cowboy as our defining myth.

CHAPTER 3

"The Acts of Their Own Hands"

Borders, Otherness, and Identity in Cormac McCarthy's *The Crossing*

> *[W]e have never been as aware as we now are of how oddly hybrid historical and cultural experiences are, of how they partake of many often contradictory experiences and domains, cross national boundaries, defy the police action of simple dogma and loud patriotism.*
>
> EDWARD SAID

Unlike *All the Pretty Horses, The Crossing* met with mixed reactions from critics. Denser, more complex, and much darker in vision (though hardly rivaling the apocalyptic horror of *Blood Meridian*), *The Crossing* continues McCarthy's exploration of myths and their relationship to culture and identity. *Blood Meridian* looked at how myths shape cultures through shaping their history and providing guidelines for how cultures will view themselves and their worlds. *All the Pretty Horses,* in turn, offered a vision of how the individual must struggle to live in the world his or her cultural myths have created. *The Crossing* moves even deeper into metaphysical questions about the role of myths as shapers of cultures and cultures as shapers of identity, especially in a world increasingly hybridized and globalized. I will argue that, much as Theodore Roosevelt moved the historic frontier and its accompanying myth out of the realm of the physical and geographic and into the far more potent realm of political symbolism, McCarthy moves the Mexican American borderlands out of the Southwest (or el norte, depending on your point of view) and into the equally potent and dangerous realm of human identities. Through the doubled figures of Billy and Boyd, the frontiers they cross, and the borderlands they inhabit, McCarthy explores a liminal space both actual and metaphorical in which subjectivity and identity are immanently self reflexive and shifting.

The Crossing deliberately invokes the iconography and mythic underpinnings of the classic Western in order to subvert and utilize them in questioning the power of borders, the pollution of those who cross them, and their roles in the structuring of identity and Otherness on the level of the national and the personal.

The genre of the Western, containing as it does a sort of ready-made insistence concerning questions of liminality, identity, and conquest, has not often, before McCarthy, fully realized those possibilities. The problems of constructing a genre built around such disturbing sites have been discussed at length by many critics. Henry Nash Smith outlined the contradictions of the Western novel as western in *Virgin Land,* claiming that by the publication of the Deadwood Dick series in 1877, the hero of the Western novel had been transformed "from a Leatherstocking with an infallible sense of right and wrong and feelings which 'appeared to possess the freshness and nature of the forest' into a man who had once been a bandit" (119), and finally into a Pinkerton-type detective who had ceased to be truly "western." These changes in the character of the Western hero, along with the growing popularity of improbable Amazon heroines who could ride, shoot, and curse with the men, resulted, according to Smith, in the Western losing "whatever chance it might once have had to develop social significance" (119). The inherent paradox, as he defined it, is that while the Leatherstocking character and those like him were objects of great popular interest, they were nonetheless loners, men who cut themselves off from significant interaction with their societies, and therefore a genre built around such a character could never adequately establish any truly complex or meaningful relationship with its society, any more than could the sensational though equally antisocial gunfighter-bandits of later works. At the same time, he wrote, the theme of "communion with nature in the West proved too flimsy to sustain a primitivistic literature of any magnitude" (119).

The pollution of those Western characters who left their own societies to cross the social, racial, and/or geographic boundaries of the frontier or who chose to willingly inhabit the liminal spaces of borderlands proved too challenging for most writers to deal with other than in a dime-novel format. Ironically, this development served a dual purpose. The inherent issues involved in Western novels (power and pollution, cultural, racial, and class conflicts, conquest and colonization of native cultures and the natural world) proved fascinating to the American public, but their generally facile treatment allowed the genre to become both immensely popular and influential in shaping and reflecting public attitudes and at the same time allowed for the masking of those same issues, permitting them to be molded, veiled, and disguised in a generally unquestioned and stereotypic form.

What McCarthy has done, beginning with *Blood Meridian* and continuing in *All the Pretty Horses* and *The Crossing,* is to subvert the genre from within, to present the familiar, comforting mask while forcing readers to recognize it *as* mask. McCarthy utilizes what Nash Smith saw as the Western's inherent weaknesses as a means for conducting a metaphysical inquiry into the nature of human society and the relationship of the individual to himself and his culture(s). By anchoring his works within the still-contested spaces of the Southwest borderlands, McCarthy is able to allude to the historic and cultural forces continually at work there and to endow his border-crossing characters with the long and paradoxical lineage inherent in his chosen genre. At the same time, he demonstrates how the politically created borderlands of the postmodern world, the sites at which nations and cultures are brought into uncomfortable intimacy as a result of imperialism, have followed the historic frontier into a mythic cyberspace where borders are at once powerfully symbolic and essentially meaningless—uncontrollable even by those governments or social structures most interested in enforcing them. It is in such a liminal postmodern space, McCarthy suggests, that identity is constructed, both within and against the myths that shape it.

The fight, first to enter a liminal space and then to leave it and rejoin some previous social order, is central in McCarthy's Western works. It is evident in the Bible-carrying kid's ironic rescue attempt of the dead peregrina in *Blood Meridian* (a woman he would have scalped without a second thought in his days with Glanton and the judge), in John Grady's mournful realization in *Pretty Horses* that the land he has returned to is no longer his, and in Billy's compulsive crossing and re-crossing of the Mexican American border. As they all discover, however, once one has been in the borderlands, or perhaps more properly come to recognize that all the world is simply a construction of borders, one is forever marked with both power and pollution.

Richard Slotkin points out that in the history of the American West and the Western novel, the Other has almost always been defined racially. Literary and historic personages like Mary Rowlandson and the other "captivity girls" or the Leatherstocking-Boone-Carson figures, who engage in intimate contact with the dark-skinned Other, are seen as simultaneously heroes in what Slotkin calls the savage war and as polluted themselves, both insiders and outsiders.[1] They are what Trinh Min-Ha identifies as "inappropriate Others," a concept she developed after the critical outrage evoked by her decision to begin making documentary films of African women, outside Southeast Asia. Was she now viewing these women as an insider or an outsider, white critics demanded? As a native of the third world or as a sophisticated and educated Western filmmaker? From what position did an Asian woman think she could speak about Africans? For Anglos especially, Trinh says, she had severely problematized the subjectivity-objectivity paradigm and somehow become both at once, inhabiting some interstitial place. She was, she says, an "inappropriate Other," more disturbing in her likeness to Anglos than in her difference from them.

The figure of the inappropriate Other, one who has transgressed beyond his or her appropriate space, out of the safe and the contained into the marginal and dangerous, abounds in the Western. Like Rowlandson or the "man-who-knows-Indians," these figures have traditionally served as a sort of uneasy negotiation or compromise in the popular imagination of the contradictory nature of frontiers, borderlands, and the power and pollution they offer.[2] They have remained vital characters in the National Symbolic for over a hundred years precisely because they both point to, and mask, the inherent contradictions in the patriotic versions of National Fantasy and national(ist) myth in which they play the starring role.

Like many Western novelists, Western historian Frederick Jackson Turner presents us with the figure of the white frontiersman who initially dons the buckskin of the Indian to enter the wilderness but who pulls "civilization" after him and is eventually able to return to a place of cultural purity free from the taint of Indianness and savagery where he can again dress in the garb of the white man, changed by his frontier experience only to the extent that he can now practice American-style democracy. However, his penetration of the frontier, his contact and mixing (racially and culturally) with the dark skinned Other, has ensured that he has no place of cultural purity to which to return. Not only is the frontiersman now an inappropriate Other, but despite its protestations, so is the culture that followed him. Within the traditional Western, authors often tried to solve this embarrassing problem by having the tainted male hero marry a genteel white woman in the end, thus bringing him back into the fold of imagined cultural purity. In the case of the wild female heroine, often raised by Indians but really a white woman underneath, authors tried marrying her to a genteel white man after a suitable decontamination period in a finishing school for young ladies back East (a site, in its supposed removal from the physical presence of a frontier, somehow more culturally innocent) once her true and pure racial identity is discovered.[3]

What these strained solutions cannot entirely disguise, however, is that neither side of a penetrated border can ever again be entirely pure. As Mary Douglas noted, social constructions have always included borders, external boundaries, and margins meant to contain the individual and to preserve the purity of those on one or the other side. In *Purity and Danger*, Douglas explains that "The danger which is risked by boundary transgression is power. Those vulnerable margins and those attacking forces which threaten to destroy good order represent the powers inhering in the cosmos" (161). "To have been in the margins," she concludes, "is to have been in contact with danger, to have been at a source of power" (97). It is also to have been in the realm of the forbidden, the polluted, and the impure.

The struggle to unite these contradictions is evident in much Western writing and the contradictory mythic heroes these texts have traditionally produced. McCarthy's works, like many Westerns before them, paradoxically depend on the existence of borders and, at the same time, on their penetration. While the outer form of the frontier myth is predicated on a postcolonial nostalgia that presumes a dominant culture both innocent of intention and, after the initial unfortunate but necessary contact involved in conquest, innocent also of any mark of the Other, within McCarthy's work one can see explored and mapped the mark retained by the colonizer from the act of colonization, of the now polluted and impure status of the dominant culture. *The Crossing* illuminates the dangerous and powerful ways this state shapes individual identity, suggesting a dialogic relationship between myths and the nations and citizens that produce and are produced by them.

If one examines the status of Mexico and Mexicans as racial Others in McCarthy's work, one can see that the mark of the Other penetrates Anglo culture more and more as the experience of the historic frontier of *Blood Meridian* recedes into the past and the semi-permanent borderlands of *All the Pretty Horses* and *The Crossing* take its place. Identity, belonging, the traditional bonds of family, culture, language, and home that define and reify the state of purity in the frontier myth are deconstructed by McCarthy, evoked then mocked, painfully and poignantly problematized through Billy and Boyd's fate in the land of their grandmother.

Borders function here on multiple levels, and their evolution can be traced through McCarthy's previous Western works. Like the significant but essentially meaningless international boundary line the wolf crosses in order to leave Mexico and enter New Mexico, borders are often ephemeral, yet more than real, defining everything while separating nothing. In *Blood Meridian*, physical borders are of little importance. The boundary between Mexico and the United States is virtually nonexistent, and crossing it does not immediately change much. To the kid, Mexico is no more strange, alien, or dangerous than New Orleans or Galveston. Crossing into Mexico simply echoes the crossing into savagery and violence that Glanton and the judge are leading, although their crossing, like Captain White's invasion and the slaughter of the Mexicans, does function as a historico-political comment on American imperialism. Glanton and his gang become alien and savage, not because they cross the Mexican border, but because they cross some other, more metaphysical border toward which, it is implied, they have been traveling all along. Rather than becoming savage by entering Mexico, they seem to bring savagery to Mexico, dragging it in their wake in the antithesis of the civilizing progress of Turner's frontiersman or Cooper's Leatherstocking.

In *Pretty Horses,* the border with Mexico is more distinctly marked and the crossing of it more definite. At the same time, however, the presence of Mexico on the U.S. side of the border and within Anglo culture is much stronger than in *Blood Meridian,* where only the semi-mythical figure of the judge, for instance, speaks fluent Spanish. John Grady in *Pretty Horses* has been taught the language by a family servant he calls abuela (grandmother), while *The Crossing* opens with Billy carrying the infant Boyd in his arms, Mexico symbolically visible in the distance, naming for his brother "the features of the landscape and birds and animals in both spanish and english" (1). Billy and Boyd's maternal grandmother was Mexican, we are told, and Boyd's twin sister, who died at age five, carries her Spanish name.

Mexico then is more than simply the savage Other, a role it has played in many Westerns; it is an inappropriate Other, more disturbing in its closeness to Billy and Boyd than in its distance from them. Crossing into Mexico is both a trip into the exotic and unknown and a return to tantalizingly familiar roots, to the cultural home of their grandmother and the corridos she taught them, which ironically seem to be the only memory of their home north of the border to bring them comfort in their times of greatest need. And like all things that must be known in McCarthy's world, Mexico, the Otherness within and the Otherness without, must be known through stories. Mexico and Mexicans here are the source of an endless stream of narratives, spinning up the world, the dangerous spaces within it, the sites of power and pollution.

Billy's first crossing is centered on a common trope in the traditional myth of the frontier and one that appears in all of McCarthy's works—the difficulty of human relationships with the natural world. This first crossing is bracketed by two main narratives given to Billy as maps both into and out of the liminal space he enters in his quest to capture, then release, the wolf, a living symbol of wild nature. The first is from the old Mexican wolf hunter Don Arnulfo who tells him that men cannot know what wolves know because only wolves understand that "there is no order in the world save that which death has put there" (45). The reason men do not understand the world or the power of a hunter and the blood he sheds is because the world lies unseen between their acts and their ceremonies. "They see the acts of their own hands or they see that which they name and call out to one another," he tells Billy, "but the world between is invisible to them" (46). Culture, in other words, constructed for humans by the myths they tell themselves about it, mediates between human perceptions and the reality of the physical world. What's more, try as men might to grasp the world through the trapped body of the wolf, they cannot. All that is left in the trap is teeth and fur. As a snowflake disappears in a clenched fist, so the wolf does also. "If you want to see it [a snowflake] you have to see it on its own ground. If you catch it you lose it. And where it goes there is no coming back from. Not even God can bring it back. . . . The wolf is made the way the world is made. You cannot touch the world. You cannot hold it in your hand for it is made of breath only" (46). This characterization of the natural world, as tantalizing yet just out of reach, as a fragile site of power and danger, foreshadows the challenge Billy will face of successfully entering such a forbidden zone and the consequences of doing so.

Billy's father attempts to know the world through the technology of the wolf trap itself, literally looking through the artifact of culture, "holding the trap at eyelevel against the morning sky he looked to be truing some older, some subtler instrument. Astrolabe or sextant. Like a man bent at fixing himself someway in the world. Bent on trying by arc or chord the space between his being and the world that was" (22). But he is unsuccessful at touching that which the wolf accesses directly and with ease. In the end Billy ignores his father's advice and the warnings of Don Arnulfo and goes to see the wolf on its own ground, to put aside the ceremonies and namings of man and to truly see the world directly. The result of course is that he succeeds in catching the wolf in a trap dug in the vaqueros' fire pit—wild nature imprisoned in the machinations of man.

But once he has seen the wolf's world, or the world as the wolf sees it, he finds, as Don Arnulfo had warned, that to return from that place is not so easy. Human culture has become for Billy transparent, or, put another way, culture has suddenly made itself visible to him, and now that he knows it is there, he no longer trusts it, can no longer abandon himself to the visions and interpretations it presents to him. Nature, however, is equally strange and untrustworthy. Like all of McCarthy's Western novels, wild nature here is at once the Other and the self, the Other contained within the self, and having entered fully into it, the self is forever changed, marked, polluted from having been in the place of power and danger from which one is normally isolated and protected by the acts and ceremonies, the myths, of men. Don Arnulfo's narrative guides Billy to the point of entry into that world, but once there he finds that his acts no longer have the power they did before, just as John Grady's naive certainty about himself and his world is shattered forever by the revelation of the hollow myth that constructed it.

The wolf, caught in the realm of acts and ceremonies, dies, becoming as Don Arnulfo predicted, simply fur and teeth. After Billy kills her and carries her body, with the baby wolves crying mutely inside her, back into the mountains for burial, he wanders deeper and deeper into the wilderness. The environmental implications of course are clear, echoing the devastated natural world of the plain of the bone pickers at the close of *Blood Meridian*.[4] This wolf, we are told time and time again, is the last wolf in the area, north or south of the border, all the others hunted to extinction like the buffalo and bears in *Blood Meridian* and the wild horses of *Pretty Horses*. With her dies some essential part of wild nature and all the wolves who might have come after her. As Billy reflects, "When those eyes and the nation to which they stood witness were gone at last with their dignity back into their origins there would perhaps be other fires and other witnesses and other worlds otherwise beheld. But they would not be this one" (74).

This guilty nostalgia for a lost world, and the conception of it in the form of a violated female (human or otherwise), is, according to Annette Kolodny, typical of American literature grown from what she terms the American Pastoral, reflecting the Anglo response to the American continent experienced as land-as-woman. She notes that "in destroying the landscape that had once promised virtually every satisfaction men have sought, men simultaneously destroy something precious, desirable and vulnerable within themselves. . . . To such dreams, the wilderness had once catered" (144). But as Henry Nash Smith noted, the theme of communion with nature in the West is not sufficient in and of itself to sustain a literature. McCarthy's characters seek, however futilely, some balance between the world of nature and the world of man, between myths and reality, acts and ceremonies, and the ephemeral truth they seem to mask. His characters seek to live on both sides of the border at once, and like the settlers Kolodny identifies as emigrating to a new and virgin landscape in order to find renewal through its possession but who then discover that settlement and possession require the destruction of the very qualities which drew them, so McCarthy's characters find that success in penetrating and inhabiting borders both fulfills and destroys them.

After the burial of the wolf, Billy lives feral in the mountains, hunting with a homemade bow and encountering no other humans for months. He is literally and figuratively lost in the wilderness, caught in the liminal place from which Don Arnulfo warned even God could not return him. In most standard Westerns, redemption would come in the form of a good woman or, less commonly, not at all, leaving the hero, like Leatherstocking, mournfully fleeing the encroaching civilization he is now too marked to rejoin.[5]

For McCarthy, redemption is a much more complex proposition. It is a second narrative that partially guides Billy out of the wilderness, though it originates from a figure usually more closely identified with the pollution of the Other than with redemption or return. Tarahumara Indians "fed him and the women washed his clothes and mended them and sewed his boots with a homemade awl and ligaments from a hawk's foot" (133), demonstrating, perhaps, one possible, albeit fragile, balance between human culture and the natural world. As Billy leaves them, an elderly man tells him that although he is an orphan he must cease his wandering in the wilderness and remake a place for himself in the world of men and that although it "seemed a place which contained men it was in reality a place contained within them and therefore to know it one must . . . live with men and not simply pass among them" (134).

As Don Arnulfo's narrative was a guide for Billy into the powerful and dangerous world of the wolf and wild nature, so the Tarahumara's is a map for crossing back into the world of ceremonies, naming, and myth and in fact implies that world is created by men through these cultural artifacts. There is a promise of a return to purity here, of escape from the pollution of being on the other side of the border and redemption through the knowledge of the world "as it existed in men's hearts" (134). It is an empty promise for Billy, however, and one he is never able to realize. His return to the United States and his second crossing into Mexico, this time with Boyd, is his attempt to somehow make good on that promise, to erase the marks of pollution by putting things right again, by returning to a time of imagined innocence and wholeness before the transgression of forbidden boundaries. If he cannot bring back his dead parents, he can try to bring back his dead parents' horses. But again he does not heed the warning given by his Tarahumara guide who reminds him that while the world of men does not contain men but rather exists in their hearts and that Billy and the world were one, "like all good things it was also a danger" (134).

Once McCarthy has introduced Boyd, effectively doubling Billy, he presents two contradictory approaches to the problem of reentering culture once that world has been exposed as a fragile borderland spun from words and myths. In imagining the Southwestern borderlands in their dual function as both separating and joining the United States and Mexico, McCarthy further problematizes the issue by doubling the number of possible human cultures to be entered and therefore to be marked by and alienated from. He suggests that the world is not only created by humans through their cultures and cultures through myths but that culture itself exists only at a doubled remove. As the old Mormon tells Billy, the acts of a single man, alone in the forbidden frontiers separated from his fellow men, have no meaning. "Acts have their being in witness" (154), he insists. In other words, if a tree falls in the forest and no one is there to hear it, it might make a sound, but the sound has no significance because it cannot be interpreted through the language of myth.

Some readers have noted that at this point *The Crossing* seems to become two separate stories: the capture and death of the wolf, followed by Billy and Boyd's adventures as outlaws in Mexico. I would argue that McCarthy is merely doubling the metaphorical problem of the power and pollution of border crossing he poses in the wolf episode, emphasizing that the figure of "the lone male in the wilderness," as Kolodny calls it, indeed represents one intransigent human problem—that of man as part of and trespasser within the world of nature—but that all humans are also part of human cultures, both at home in and outlaws within the world of words and acts shaped by human myths. Just as the kid helped bring forth a new culture in *Blood Meridian* and found that he had to join it or die, and as John Grady searched for a way to reenter his own culture once it has been stripped bare for him of the myths that structured it, so Billy and Boyd battle to resynthesize their vision of themselves and the world once they learn the truth of it according to the primadonna: that in this world the mask is the truth (229), and the mediating mask of myth and culture does not hide reality but creates it. Unlike wolves who can touch the world directly, McCarthy seems to suggest that humans must have culture to see through, must have myths in order to have something to see; otherwise they are orphans, and their acts, without witness, have no being.

Possessing this knowledge marks the boys with power and pollution, as evidenced by the townsfolk's contradictory response to Billy: "people passing in the street turned to look at him. Something in off the wild mesas, something out of the past. . . . Totally unspoken for. In that outlandish figure they beheld what they envied most and what they most reviled. If their hearts went out to him it was yet true that for very small cause they might also have killed him" (170). Billy has become a double of the mythic Western hero, feared and envied, insider and outsider, an inappropriate Other marked by his transgression of a border at once ubiquitous and desperately ignored and, most disturbingly, still part of the culture through which he moves. As the primadonna tells the boys, the secret she knows is not only that in this world the mask is the truth, but that is also the secret for which she must be killed on stage each night, a border crosser punished for possession of the forbidden knowledge that the border is always already within the very culture and cultural constructs that attempt to enforce it.

Billy is now neither fully a part of the world of men nor wholly part of nature, alien in both the United States and Mexico, caught, even, between life and death. Like the man tragically spared in the old Mormon's story, he is a "trunk without root or branch" (146). His liminal status is reified in his exchange with the Mexican woman who brings him menudo after his night in the tavern. She studies his hand like a fortune-teller, and when Billy asks what she sees there, she replies, "dos hermanos. . . . Uno que vive, uno que ha muerto" [two brothers. . . . one that lives, one that has died]. Billy asks, tellingly, "Cual es cual?" [which is which?] (369), recognizing subconsciously that he is the brother who has died, seeing himself as having "no prior life. As if he had died in some way years ago" (382).

McCarthy poses this problem as symbolic of the contradiction of a borderlands existence in a modern world culturally hybridized through centuries of imperialism, a place where all cultures have become borderlands cultures, mixed and impure. The clear boundary between Mexican and American, like that between life and death, has become blurred. While Billy remains physically alive, Boyd has died twice in Mexico and twice been revived by los hombres del país, first symbolically after he is shot and nursed back to health and again after his actual death and subsequent rebirth in the corridos sung on both sides of the border. Boyd has entered the world of men by entering the culture and myths of Mexico, something Billy refuses to do, as he is ultimately refused entry in America when he tries to join the army. Boyd remains marked, an outlaw, always an inappropriate Other even within Mexico, but his Otherness is embraced by la gente del país, offering him a symbolic, if physically short-lived, redemption that escapes Billy.

Contrary to what is commonly imagined in standard Westerns, Boyd's redemption does not represent any kind of return to an imagined cultural purity, an act impossible in a hybridized world. His impure identity as signifier of the impurity of both (all) cultures on both sides of the international border must inevitably be labeled as monstrous by those societies. In attempts to deal with such troubling contradictions, many cultures have assigned special significance to those marked with pollution. Douglas explains the power of boundary crossing figures: "Whenever a strict pattern of purity is imposed on our lives it is either highly uncomfortable or it leads into contradiction . . . . That which is negated is not thereby removed. The rest of life, which does not tidily fit the accepted categories, is still there and demands attention. . . . And as life must be affirmed, the most complete philosophies, as William James put it, must find some ultimate way of affirming that which has been rejected" (163–64).

The power of borders and their primary function is to ensure the purity of those enclosed within one or both categories and to prevent the pollution sure to occur if those contained on one side of the equation move out of their boundary, crossing margins and mixing with those similarly imprisoned on the other side. Boyd, as outlaw and saint, Mexican and American, dead brother and immortal hero, affirms the power of pollution and monstrousness, the strength of impurity, by existing both as product and symbol of crossed borders and mixed cultures. He is McCarthy's postmodern version of the mythic frontier hero, signifying at once the mask and the truth within and beneath it. The irony for McCarthy is that the only figure to successfully achieve this balance must die in the process, as the primadonna dies each night on stage.[6]

Boyd's entry into the corridos of the country people as a mythic hero signifies McCarthy's vision of the power of myths to shape the world and the identities of humans who inhabit it. We never hear exactly how Boyd died, though the implication is that he was shot in a futile quest for justice for the peasants who once nursed him back to health. As Billy rides through the countryside after his third and final crossing seeking news of Boyd, he first hears the corrido that has been created about his brother "in which the young güero comes down from the north. Pelo tan rubio. Pistola en mano" [Hair so blond. Pistol in hand] (375). The phrases are mythic in nature, at once particular and formulaic, and this corrido is later conflated with other, older songs the boys have heard earlier, both in Mexico and the United States, adding the Mexican girl as Boyd's sister/lover/twin and tying them into the tradition of mythic heroes, soldaderas and güeros, dying young and yet living on through their roles as mythic signifiers for their cultures. The singers of the corridos have made of Boyd's life the myth that will best serve their needs as inappropriate Others in their own world, in the words of Douglas, affirming that which has been rejected.

In this way, the corridos about the frontier/borderlands figure serve much the same function as the figure itself: negotiating forbidden and disturbing terrain while still masking in stereotypical and appropriate forms the history and conditions that make the terrain forbidden and its inhabitants polluted and monstrous, conquered and impure Others. The center of the novel has in fact become neither one side nor the other of the Mexican American border but rather a mobile, unfixed borderlands region, continually betwixt and between possible worlds.

This is, of course, also the situation of Billy. Like the kid's futile attempt to reverse the course of the myth he helped bring into being in *Blood Meridian,* Billy tries to reverse the course of events he set into motion by his decision to cross the forbidden frontier into the world of the wolf (or his decision to enter Mexico with it, or his Mexican grandmother's decision to marry an Anglo, or any of the other acts of history and colonization that have led to this point). But like the frontiersman's attempt to return to a state of cultural purity, before contact or conquest, it is an impossible task.

Unable to accept his existence in such a state, Billy's final crossing is a mournful attempt to find what Boyd has found—a place in the world—by claiming the only thing left that represents connection to the world of men for him: Boyd's bones. The exhumation of Boyd's body and the attempt to return it to what Billy supposes is the proper side of the border is a reversal of the process of the return and burial of the wolf and an equally meaningless act. There is no proper side to any border; all sides are equally monstrous, equally powerful, all extract an equal price for the knowledge that identity is polluted and purity unattainable, and yet, paradoxically, this knowledge and this impurity are what enables life to continue.

Billy discovers, as he did with the wolf, that Boyd is not in his bones but rather is living in the hearts and memories of people, leaving Billy as the dead brother. In this tragic manner, dragging his brother's decayed corpse through the wilderness, the question of identity in the borderlands is finally made clear to Billy. Boyd's identity is not in his bones but, like that of the mysterious plane, rather in his history, or more properly in the witnessing of his acts now reified and mythologized by the singers of his corridos. Billy's counterclaim to Boyd's identity, his memories and dreams of his brother, his claiming of Boyd's bones, is fruitless. Boyd's value, identity, and history exist in the hearts of all who sing his story and make of it a myth by which to shape their lives.

The gypsy tries to explain this to Billy by explaining the significance of photos of people dead for decades that he, like his father, sells from the back of their wagon: "What he came to see was that as the kinfolk in their fading stills could have no value save in another's heart so it was with that heart also in another's in a terrible and endless attrition and of any other value there was none" (413). Billy's value lay only in the heart of Boyd. He never successfully joins any culture on either side of the border; therefore his identity, anchored only in nature but not in the world of ceremonies and naming, is trapped in the space between himself and his actions, between the world and its creation in ritual and myth. He has entered the borderlands and now cannot find a way out again, and, unlike Boyd, neither can he find a way to live within them or perhaps is unwilling to pay the price Boyd and the primadonna pay.

This tragic paradox, the extremity of the price to be paid to find a way to live in the postmodern borderlands, is consistent throughout McCarthy's Western works. There is a demand implicit in them that we acknowledge the truth in the mythic masks we place upon our culture's border crossers, those figures of fear and envy upon whom the National Symbolic has depended to render palatable those contradictions in history, culture, and society we choose not to see. From the mythic figure of the sacred hunter perverted in *Blood Meridian* to its rebirth as the sacred cowboy in *Pretty Horses* to Billy's hopeless search for purity and return, McCarthy implicates the culture and the icons it has chosen to accept, and the truths it has chosen to disguise, in charging that the world we live in is created in our own hearts and minds.

CHAPTER 4

Decolonizing Imperialism

Captivity Myths and the Postmodern World in Leslie Marmon Silko's *Ceremony*

> *[C]ultural identities have histories. . . . they undergo constant transformation and . . . far from being etched in the past, cultural identities are constantly being constructed.*
>
> ANGIE CHABRAM AND ROSA LINDA FREGOSO

The frontier myth, as it functions for Anglo America, can be seen as a set of hero tales modeling morally justified acts of violence meant to assert and maintain the dominance of a favored class and race. The works of Cormac McCarthy illustrate how powerfully this myth shapes the beliefs and attitudes of white Americans. In *Ceremony,* Leslie Marmon Silko utilizes the same mythic narrative to interrogate the ways in which the process of imperialism takes place beyond the level of laws and guns, examining how it is maintained and the impact it has in constructing the identity of Native Americans. She explores methods of cultural and economic conquest and control of native people as well as the devastating consequences of it. This is a vision of the frontier myth seen from the other side of the frontier, so to speak, but a side equally driven and shaped by the compelling narrative this myth presents.

While it may seem odd to imagine a Native American writer producing a Western, I argue that is exactly what Silko has done, although in a deliberately subversive manner. No groups, least of all colonized people, are free from the influence of the mythic narratives that direct the formation of identity in the United States. That does not mean, however, they are powerless to challenge these narratives. Simply by writing and publishing, a native writer subverts the intent of the frontier myth to silence and erase the subaltern group. Nonetheless, Silko, like nearly all Americans, was educated within the framework of a dominant culture guided by the frontier myth and the Western as its most obvious vehicle. While scores of works have examined Silko as Native American writer, and nearly as many have engaged her as feminist writer, none have really addressed her as *Western* writer.[1] By this, I mean to look at her work from two directions—both as texts produced from and about the geographic space commonly known as the American West and as texts that are heir to the tradition labeled Western literature, that is to say operating within many of the commonly recognized tropes, symbols, and forms associated with that genre. Silko herself acknowledges the literary influence of both native and nonnative authors, especially that of her close friend, Western writer Larry McMurtry.[2]

Many scholars have traced the evolution of Western literature from Cooper, particularly his Leatherstocking series. But as they have also noted, Cooper grew out of the New England literary tradition that dealt with the frontier primarily through the vehicle of captivity narratives. Richard Slotkin calls the captivity narrative the "archetype of the American experience" (*Regeneration Through Violence,* 98) and notes that from 1682 to 1716 "captivities were the only narratives about the frontier published in America" (144). Annette Kolodny claims the captivity narratives resonated so powerfully with Anglo audiences because they invoked the pathos-laden vision of "*Judea capta,* Israel suffering in Babylonian captivity" (*The Lay of the Land,* 19) and were therefore sympathetic to an Anglo American public that viewed itself not as aggressors or invaders on the various Western frontiers but as innocent victims of unprovoked attacks endured as they strove to carry out the holy mission of Manifest Destiny placed before them by God.

In the nineteenth century, abolitionists, both black and white, were able to turn this emotional response to their advantage by presenting slavery as a kind of African captivity narrative, thus providing an early example of the flexibility of this literary form. Captivity narratives in various guises remained popular throughout the eighteenth, nineteenth, and twentieth centuries, influencing the structure and themes of much American literature, especially that from and about the West, be it imagined as the wilds of Kentucky, the Great Plains, or the Southwestern deserts. The captivity narrative can be seen as both a precursor to and subgenre of the Western.

With the exception of abolitionist texts, however, captivity narratives have nearly always presented innocent whites at the mercy of savage Indians. But while we may normally think of captivity narratives as an exclusively Anglo phenomenon, Slotkin notes that many New England tribes also had traditions, rituals, and narratives revolving around the experiences of captivity.

Though Silko is, of course, a member of Laguna Pueblo, not an eastern tribe, the elements that gave rise to both the Puritan and Indian captivity narratives in New England are exclusive to neither that region nor to the seventeenth or eighteenth centuries. Captivity narratives are essentially a response to a frontier situation, stories generated to engage and resolve one culture or group's precarious existence in the face of a hostile enemy threatening from the opposite side of some border (geographic, racial, cultural). The captivity narrative can be seen as a sort of condensation of the myths a culture generates from and about its frontier regions and thus provides a particularly rich site from which to examine the process of mythogenesis.

Traditional Anglo American captivity literature generally preferred to see whites as vulnerable but brave pioneers beset by wild savages, and this original Puritan blueprint followed Anglo settlement westward through the eighteenth and nineteenth centuries, adapting itself to the changing social, political, and cultural realities of constantly shifting frontiers. The Puritan captivity narrative evolved into the Western through the gradual evolution of the hero and his or her response to the frontier situation. Mary Rowlandson, author and subject of the first Anglo captivity narrative in New England, thus gave way to Cooper's Leatherstocking, who in turn became Boone, Crockett, Carson, and their innumerable modern variations, from Dead Eye Dick and the Virginian to Marshal Dillon and the Texas Rangers (beset by savage outlaws and swarthy Mexicans rather than Indians). The trail leading from Mary Rowlandson to McCarthy's kid proceeds something like this: Hero as Indian captive became hero as Indian-like hunter who became hero as Indian killer, often circling directly back to the captivity narratives of old by rescuing a white captive (usually a woman or feminized Eastern man) from the appropriate savage Other.

Silko has carried that archetypal hero forward until hero becomes Indian. The Anglo captivity narrative as archetype of the Anglo American experience becomes the archetype of Native American experience, as well. In *Ceremony,* Silko creates a modern Indian captivity narrative by remaking the traditional myths of both Native American and Anglo American cultures, a process Edward Said claims is common for the decolonizing native writer.[3] Silko highlights the deep structures of symbol and value inherent in each cultures' myths by pushing those elements beyond their common boundaries into new contexts, thereby forcing new visions of traditional myths and new perspectives of old figures. She pushes these boundaries to such an extent one may argue she essentially creates a new myth. Just as McCarthy's reenvisioned sacred hunter marks a change not only in the outer form of the myth (an evolution of the hero and his universe to be expected with the passage of time), Silko also creates a new myth out of the bones of the old. Such a profound change in mythic structure, as Slotkin notes, reflects more than simply a modernization of a traditional narrative or story; it indicates a "fundamental alteration of the culture's conception of the relationship of man to the universe, a revolution in world view, cosmology, historical and moral theory, and self-concept" (*Regeneration Through Violence*, 9).

Ceremony details just such a sea change through the form of the captivity narrative but with profound alterations of the mythic structures underlying it. Paula Gunn Allen claims that Native American authors who choose to write novels that follow western (nonnative) themes and plot conventions "find themselves restricted to stories that center on loss of identity, loss of cultural self-determination, genocide or deicide, and cultural clash" (81). Silko moves beyond this restriction, however, by inscribing cultural and mythic change across not only Pueblo and Navajo cultures but traditional Mexican and Anglo cultural myths as well, reflecting the postmodern reality of hybridized traditions, mixed races, and crossed borders. *Ceremony* is neither entirely Indian-based nor completely western but a hybrid of both. In it, Silko examines how imperialism is maintained and enforced while setting forth a model of decolonization, a mythic narrative illustrating how imperialism may be subverted by a subaltern group even when the confines of imperial reality can never be entirely escaped.

Like McCarthy's Western fiction, much of Silko's writing is also a reference to and deconstruction of the rhetoric of National Fantasy and the structures of the National Symbolic. These entities may be generated mainly by Anglo Americans, but their influence is by no means limited to white males. Anyone living in America will have internalized much of the lessons they purport to teach, as Tayo realizes when he examines his own unwillingness to believe a white man could be guilty of stealing cattle despite obvious evidence to the contrary: "He knew then he had learned the lie by heart—the lie which they had wanted him to learn: only brown-skinned people were thieves" (191). The success of America's cultural imperialism has ensured that no child, white or brown, Anglo or Indian, can grow up without the shadow of that mythic history coloring their perceptions of self and Other. In *Ceremony,* Silko harnesses the guilt, fear, and anxiety of a captive culture and moves it toward a mythical moment of redemption and release.

Captivity narratives, regardless of when or where they are generated, have certain elements in common. They generally begin with a brief excerpt from a religious text and proceed with the intent to teach their audience an important spiritual lesson. The captive, and often his or her community, is seen as existing in a state of spiritual isolation and peril on the frontier, outcast from their own land. As a result of captivity, the victim is lost to the community until his or her rescue or escape. The community's response to the redeemed captive is to rally around the victim in a ceremony or ritual and, especially in Puritan and New England Indian cultures, to exalt the victim "to a level equivalent to members of the medicine society, with the task of witchfinding (an honored profession among the Indians)" (*Regeneration through Violence,* 137).[4] In later Westerns, the ritual often took the form of a wedding ceremony, safely uniting the redeemed white captive with a proper white representative of his, or more often her, community, thus negating the threat of cultural, racial, or sexual assimilation. In both Indian and Anglo societies, however, the function of captivity narratives was the same: to express a culture's anxieties about its real or imagined helplessness in the face of a savage Other, then attempt to resolve those anxieties through redemption and salvation.

Silko begins her story of captivity and redemption in *Ceremony* with the invocation of a religious text on the first page. Ts'its'tsi'nako, Thought-Woman, sometimes called Grandmother Spider, is the central creation figure in Pueblo tradition and in Navajo myths as well. Just as Mary Rowlandson opened her narrative with a Biblical passage and liberally salted her story with further quotes to serve as spiritual guideposts for her audience, Silko commences by introducing Thought-Woman and her sisters in the sacred act of creation. But in a doubling of the use to which most Anglo writers put Biblical scriptures, Silko invokes Thought-Woman as creating not only the world but the text itself.

Thought-Woman, the spider
named things and
as she named them
they appeared.

She is sitting in her room
thinking of a story now
I'm telling you the story
she is thinking. (1)

This passage functions on several levels. It cues the reader that the story they are about to engage with is in the nature of a spiritual quest, more than mere entertainment. It also carries to a heightened level the goal of most captivity narratives: the participation and redemption of the audience along with the captive, through the shared experience of the captive's story. Silko implies her audience is so closely tied to the experience of the narrative, the story is literally taking place as the reader turns the pages. The reader is thus implicated in the act of the narrative's unfolding as both active participant and chosen instrument of the author/creator, Thought-Woman, who at least partly directs the actions of the story.

And this narrative is no ordinary story. If we have not yet figured out from the title of the book what this narrative is about, Silko tells us on the next page, which begins with the single word, "ceremony" (2). The book functions as a conflation of both the story of the captive and the community's ritual or ceremonial response to his or her return. The narrative here becomes the ceremony, and the audience is guided in their participation though the act of reading it and by the ceremonial signposts in the form of the mythic, semi-religious verses Silko sets up along the way. Each of these verses serves to either teach a lesson in the form of a modified traditional Pueblo or Navajo myth relating to the actions of the characters in the novel or to take the reader along with Tayo as he undergoes various ceremonies meant to return him to his community, to physical health, and to spiritual wholeness.

As with many captivity narratives, the captive's physical state is indicative of his condition of spiritual isolation and peril. Like his community as a whole, Tayo is alienated from himself and from his home, his spirit held in a state of deadly imprisonment by Anglo culture and the white invaders who have dispossessed the Indians of their land and worked to destroy their world. Silko demonstrates Pueblo cultural captivity and American cultural imperialism in several ways, most especially through the powerful, dominating figures of white schoolteachers. These teachers represent both the hope of escape from the poverty of the reservations through education, held out as a token to the Indians, and at the same time the destructive imperialism that has imprisoned and impoverished them in the first place. The old mythic stories told by his grandmother and uncle that Tayo cherished as a child and that are the means by which much of the children's cultural heritage is learned, are derided by the white teachers as superstitious nonsense, not even accorded respect as religious parables in the way Christian creation myths are treated:

> He knew what white people thought about the stories. In school the science teacher had explained what superstition was, and then held the science textbook up for the class to see the true source of explana-

tions. He had studied those books, and he had no reasons to believe the stories any more. (94)

> Like the first time in science class, when the teacher brought in a tubful of dead frogs, bloated with formaldehyde, and the Navajos all left the room; the teacher said those old beliefs were stupid. The Jemez girl raised her hand and said the people always told the kids not to kill frogs, because the frogs would get angry and send so much rain there would be floods. The science teacher laughed loudly, for a long time; he even had to wipe tears from his eyes. (195)

The result of such derision is not only the captivity of the children, now held by the unassailable authority of the teacher and the colonizing culture he represents, but also the disintegration of relationships within native communities at home, endangering equally those children forced to endure the science teacher's insulting laughter and their families as well. While Tayo tells himself he has no reason to believe the old stories any longer, he cannot shake the profound spiritual feeling when he is out in the natural world observing the frogs and snakes and other creatures that those old stories are still somehow true, that these Indian myths still hold the power to shape the world. Tayo retains the capacity to recognize the spiritual in the physical world, despite his cultural indoctrination at the hands of white teachers.

Tayo's cousin Rocky, however, has been thoroughly consumed by Anglo culture, succumbing, as so many captivity narratives warn against, to the veiled threats and blandishments of his captors. His captivity shakes the foundations of his entire family. When his uncle Josiah decides to begin raising cattle, he reads books on scientific methods of cattle breeding loaned to him by a BIA extension agent. Josiah finds the books unrealistic because they do not deal with many of the realities of life in the Western desert such as droughts, floods, blizzards, cactus, and thistles. He decides to abandon the books, telling Tayo and Rocky,

> "We'll have to do things our own way. Maybe we'll even write our own book, Cattle Raising on Indian Land, or how to raise cattle that don't eat grass or drink water."
>
> Tayo and Robert laughed with him, but Rocky was quiet. He looked up from his books.
>
> "Those books are written by scientists. They know everything there is to know about beef cattle. That's the trouble with the way people

around here have always done things—they never knew what they were doing." . . . He did not hesitate to speak like that, to his father and his uncle, because the subject was books and scientific knowledge—those things that Rocky had learned to believe in. . . . Auntie had been listening but she did not seem to notice Rocky's disrespect. She valued Rocky's growing understanding of the outside world, of the books, of everything of importance and power. He was becoming what she had always wanted. (76)

Rocky's captivity is a wedge separating husband and wife, father and son, sister and brother, disrupting also the important relationship in Pueblo society between maternal uncle and nephew. All Robert's and Josiah's wisdom, as older, experienced men, and what their knowledge represents for Pueblo culture, is as lost to Rocky as the importance of the traditional native myths on the science teacher. Silko implies that an important balance has been upset, not just a balance between Anglos and Indians but between Indians and Indians—a disintegration from within, illuminating the same anxieties over cultural disruption so common in Anglo captivity narratives that reflected horror at the thought of a white captive or white culture being consumed, through marriage or cannibalism, by Indians.

Rocky has been entirely colonized by the conqueror's myths. His devotion to Anglo culture and his desperate longing to be accepted by it cannot save him, however, and instead cause his death. It is Rocky's desire to prove to the white Army recruiter his right to be seen as a "real" American despite his brown skin that motivates him to volunteer for the Army during World War II. The result is his subsequent death in the Philippines. The Japanese army in the Philippines is both a double of the Anglo presence in the Americas, insofar as its presence is an act of violent colonialism, and a disturbing inversion, as Tayo recognizes when he finds he cannot bear to shoot at the Japanese soldiers whose facial features are so similar to the Lagunas'. Rocky is as much a captive of the United States as he is of the Japanese army. Both share equal responsibility for his death. In the end, Rocky literally dies in captivity, as much from being utterly consumed by Anglo culture and the frontier myth structuring it as from the effects of the Japanese grenade.

Tayo's mother, Laura, Auntie's younger sister, also dies in captivity, a victim not of desperate patriotism or enemy shrapnel but of more subtle attacks. Like her narrative twin, Helen Jean, Tayo's mother is imprisoned by Anglo culture's double vision of native women. They are seen at once as worthless due to their culture and their skin color and, at the same time, possessing value through their sexuality. But, having been sexually possessed by a white man, they are degraded even more, shamed in the eyes of both Anglo and native cultures. It is a trap from which few Native women in *Ceremony* ever escape. And the captivity of Indian women is especially devastating to Indian culture. Silko writes of Tayo's mother:

> When Little Sister had started drinking wine and riding in cars with white men and Mexicans, the people could not define their feeling about her. The Catholic priest shook his finger at the drunkenness and lust, but the people felt something deeper: they were losing her, they were losing part of themselves. The older sister had to act; she had to act for the people, to get this young girl back.
>
> It might have been possible if the girl had not been ashamed of herself. Shamed by what they taught her in school about the deplorable ways of the Indian people. (68)

As this passage demonstrates, the captivity of a single member imperils the entire community, and yet unlike the relatively simple act of redeeming Tayo from the Japanese POW camp, recovering a captive lost in the way Laura or Helen Jean is lost, engulfed in the world of their conqueror's myth, proves considerably more difficult. In fact, only a handful of older women like Auntie and Grandma, and the mystical, semi-divine Ts'eh, manage to escape this kind of deadly captivity. No other Indian woman in the novel survives.

Like Helen Jean, Tayo's mother is destroyed both by Anglo racism and by Anglo misogyny—a two-pronged attack Indian men are not subject to, and this is perhaps why they have a somewhat better survival rate in the novel than the women. Both Helen Jean and Laura become obsessed with their physical appearance as women, especially with how they can make themselves appear more white, despite the shame they know will come from their own culture if they are successful in attracting white men. Tayo's mother is "excited to see that despite the fact she was an Indian, the white men smiled at her from their cars as she walked from the bus stop in Albuquerque back to Indian School. She smiled and waved; she looked at her own reflection in windows of houses she passed; her dress, her lipstick, her hair—it was all done perfectly, the way the home-ec teacher taught them, exactly like the white girls" (69). Similarly, Helen Jean, who leaves her reservation for Albuquerque where she hopes to get a good job so she can help out the people at home, ends up working as a cheap prostitute in the local Indian bars. Nonetheless, she is still able to feel some pride in the "white" aspects of her appearance: "Her hair was cut short and was tightly curled. It needed to be washed, but at least it wasn't long or straight. She touched up her left eyebrow and put on more lipstick. . . . If she hung around any longer with these guys, that's how she'd end up. Like the rest of the Indians" (166). The last we see of Helen Jean, she has ditched Harley and Pinkie, who are broke, and has left the bar with a Mexican railroad worker who has just drawn his pay, promising herself that this time she'll put aside a little of the money she makes from him to send to her family back on the reservation. Her downward spiral is apparent and virtually identical to Laura's. Both of them, like Rocky, are lost beyond escape or redemption. They suffer the fate most feared in captivity narratives: they are cannibalized and consumed by their captor's culture.

Their loss further endangers their communities, already on the verge of shattering under the pressures of colonization. Even those who remain on the reservation, within the geographic bounds of the community, are not safe. Cultural imperialism easily violates geographic and political borders. The devoutly Christian Auntie, who dutifully attends church every Sunday, is as symbolically captive as her son or her sister. Christianity, Silko writes, "separated the people from themselves; it tried to crush the single clan name, encouraging each person to stand alone because Jesus Christ would save only the individual soul" (68). Each week, Auntie goes to church alone. Although she tells her family she prays they will be baptized, Tayo recalls that she never asks any of them, not even her own son Rocky, to accompany her. Later, Tayo wonders if "she liked it that way, going to church by herself, where she could show the people that she was a devout Christian and not immoral or pagan like the rest of the family. When it came to saving her own soul, she wanted to be careful that there were no mistakes" (77). She too is lost to her family, her clan, and her community.

Auntie's devotion to the salvation of her own soul through focusing all her spirituality on the church and the words of the white priest illustrates an important difference between Silko's captivity myth and its Anglo counterparts. As with Anglo captivity narratives, and Western literature in general, landscape and religion play a major role. Like many Anglo authors, Silko utilizes the natural world, among other things, to symbolize Tayo's spiritual sickness and his community's state of perilous captivity. Her hero is captive, however, not because he is lost in the wilderness and thus separated from the sacred but because he is lost *from* the wilderness. Within Silko's narrative, the earth is more than simply a symbolic stage upon which humans act out the drama of their individual lives or something that must be conquered by man according to the strictures of the frontier myth. In the myth systems of the Pueblos, there is a spiritual connection between land and people. Each responds to the other, and human actions can be punished or rewarded by a sacred and sentient earth. In *Ceremony,* however, the land itself is seen as captive along with the people who once enjoyed a holy relationship with it. Auntie is never mentioned in connection with any aspect of the natural world. White school teachers tell the Indian children their myths of a sacred earth and animal spirits are laughable superstition, and Auntie abandons even her own son to follow a spiritual ideal that views wilderness as the realm of the devil.

The captivity of the land is not merely metaphorical. In one scene, Tayo searches for his uncle's stolen cattle on a mountain that was once a traditional hunting ground for the Laguna people. In an illustration of the effectiveness of the legalistic aspect of imperialism, it was taken by the Forest Service and the State of New Mexico, then sold to white ranchers from Texas in the early 1900s. Silko writes that

> In the twenties and thirties the loggers had come, and they stripped the canyons below the rim and cut great clearings on the plateau slopes. The logging companies hired full-time hunters who fed entire logging camps, taking ten or fifteen deer each week and fifty wild turkeys in a single month. The loggers shot the bears and mountain lions for sport. And it was then the Laguna people understood that the land had been taken, because they couldn't stop these white people from coming to destroy the animals and the land. It was then too that the old men at Laguna and Acoma warned the people that the balance of the world had been disturbed and the people could expect droughts and harder days to come. (185–86)

While possession of land has always symbolized power in both Anglo and Indian societies, it is in her treatment of nature that Silko's captivity myth begins to differ significantly from the Anglo archetype. In the Puritan view, and in the view of most Western literature following, land not cleared and plowed was a hellish place, a howling wilderness signifying the antithesis of civilization, humanity, safety, and home. Slotkin writes that in Puritan captivity narratives, the wilderness "is seen only as a wasteland of starvation and hardship. Natural terrain is suggested in horrific abstractions, the landscape of the Puritan mind replaces the real wilderness" (99). And as symbol of the savage Indian who lived in its midst, the wilderness for the Puritans became the living incarnation of evil, the realm of the devil. Slotkin continues, "The Puritan terror of . . . Indian marriage . . . derived from their fear of allowing themselves to adjust to and merge with the environment of the New World . . . . Marriage symbolized this process of acculturation in terms of a sexual merging of the races. . . . For the Puritan, the traditional revulsion [at marriage with Indians] . . . was heightened by the horror implicit in the idea of sexual marriage with the wilderness" (125). The result is a growing Anglo belief that "the only acceptable communion between Christian and Indian, civilization and wilderness, was the communion of murder, hunger, and bloodlust" (125).

Cooper marks a reprieve in this stark vision, but it is short lived. Henry Nash Smith notes that by the late 1850s, the archetypal frontier hero had lost the Leatherstocking's "power to commune with nature. . . . He no longer looks to God through nature, for nature is no longer benign: its symbols are the wolves and the prairie fire. . . . The landscape within which the Western hero operates has become . . . 'a dreary waste.' . . . He is . . . alone in a hostile, or at best a neutral, universe" (89).

The landscape in Silko's captivity narrative, however, reverses this vision of nature, replacing it with one more closely aligned with Native American, rather than Anglo, myths. While redemption for Anglo captives meant deliverance from the wilderness, for Tayo it means reunion with it. While mythic Anglo figures like Davy Crockett and Paul Bunyan inspire the white loggers and hunters who fulfill the guidelines of the Anglo myth by conquering the wilderness, Tayo's redemption lies in restoring it. Because the Indians no longer possess the land, however, and because Indian communities have become estranged from it, this task is a monumental one, made even more difficult by the Indians' sense of guilt. As Tayo stands at Betonie's hogan above the Gallup junkyard and city dump, he looks down on the lights of Gallup sprawling across a valley once inhabited by Native Americans and remarks bitterly:

> "They took almost everything, didn't they?"
>
> The old man looked up from the fire. . . . "We always come back to that, don't we? It was planned that way. For all the anger and the frustration. And for the guilt too. Indians wake up every morning of their lives to see the land which was stolen, still there, within reach, its theft being flaunted." (127)

The land here is emblematic not only of the state of captivity of Tayo's community but of their sense of guilt as well. Silko takes great care in presenting the Indians' persecution at the hands of whites, as well as their own sense of unworthiness. This is a classic component of both Anglo and Indian captivity narratives, in which the captive and his or her community must examine the state of their own hearts. Within the Puritan-Christian worldview, the captive's plight at the hands of his or her captors mirrors the state of the captive's and the community's soul, imprisoned by sinfulness, pride, or greed. While Tayo and his community are more sinned-against than sinners here, Tayo nonetheless has an act upon his conscience that he feels to be monstrous, and his guilt for that act plays a significant role in his state of heartsick captivity.

As he staggers through the jungles of the Philippines as a prisoner of war, struggling to support Rocky's body, he begins to curse the tropical rains in a ritualistic chant, damning one of the most holy things in the Pueblo world: "When Tayo prayed on the long muddy road to the prison camp, it was for dry air, dry as a hundred years squeezed out of yellow sand, air to dry out the oozing wounds of Rocky's leg. . . . Tayo hated this unending rain as if it were the jungle green rain and not the miles of marching or the japanese grenade that was killing Rocky. . . . and he started repeating "Goddamn, goddamn!"; it flooded out of the last warm core in his chest and echoed inside his head. He damned the rain until the words were a chant, and he sang it while he crawled through the mud. . . . all the time he could hear his own voice praying against the rain" (12). Paula Gunn Allen notes that simply by being a warrior and engaging in the act of war, however unwillingly, Tayo becomes alienated from Pueblo life, because warriors "in a peace-centered culture must experience total separation from the tribe" (123). Tayo's alienation goes beyond that of a warrior, however, and his curse against the rain haunts him upon his return to Laguna. He is not the only Indian war veteran who has become separated from the community or sinned against the land. Emo, in a modern echo of the cautionary Pueblo myth of Reed Woman and Corn Woman that Silko weaves through this part of the narrative, scorns the natural world: "Emo liked to point to the restless dusty wind and the cloudless skies, to the bony horses chewing on fence posts beside the highway; Emo liked to say 'Look what is here for us. Look. Here's the Indians' mother earth! Old dried-up thing!'" (25). The result of this psychic separation and captivity is just as the old men had predicted—drought and suffering, and for the captive Tayo, a constant sense of guilt at having betrayed the land and, through it, his community.

Establishing the captive's proper relationship to his or her community is fundamental in all captivity narratives. Once redeemed from Indians and the savage wilderness, Anglo captives had to reintegrate themselves with

Christian society, often through the ceremony of marriage to a white person, in order to be rid of the taint of the wilderness and the threat of sexual communion with nature through the bodies of Indians. Tayo, on the other hand, must reintegrate himself with his community by reintegrating himself with nature through sexual communion with Nightswan and Ts'eh, representatives of the natural world.

For the Puritans, the wilderness was a signifier of evil, seducing whites away from the Christian faith and spiritual salvation with the sexual temptation of the sacred marriage of the ancient hunter myths. These mythic narratives held great sway over the Anglo imagination in the New World, and the negative connotations they had come to bear under Christianity colored Anglo perceptions of the Americas. In New England in 1653, for example, one woman was convicted and hanged for taking the Indian devil-god Hobbamock for a husband. Another confessed to fornication with devils in the shape of forest deer. The new Anglo version of the sacred hunter myth, which both instigated and grew from such incidents, attempted to demonize or erase the sacred marriage that united the hunter with the spirit of the wilderness, to see the nature spirit the hunter sought as dark and evil, rather than a source of creativity and fertility. This hatred of the symbol of nature, however, violated the ethic of the hunter myth in which the hunter and his prey are intended to respectfully share and interchange identities as the quarry the hunter follows often is discovered to be not an animal but a female avatar of nature, whom the hunter marries instead of slays in a parallel renewal of self and community.

But the idea of interchanging identities with the New World wilderness or its Indian inhabitants was anathema to early Anglo culture, which saw itself as constantly imperiled and in danger of being swallowed up by Indians and their wilderness home. Thus, Anglo captives were sternly warned against succumbing to the temptation of marriage to the wilderness through the bodies of Indians. A major theme in Anglo captivity narratives is the captive's resistance to this temptation, strengthened by the captive's Christian faith which clearly shows that evil, like Indians and devils in the form of forest deer, lurks in the wilderness. To be saved, the captive had to be redeemed from nature back into the society of God and men.

For Silko, it is the mythic sacred marriage that saves, rather than damns, the captive and his community. Tayo cannot be redeemed until he has achieved sexual union with nature. The wilderness, instead of being a place of exile from the sacred, truly godforsaken, is both the site and source of holiness. By damning the rain and alienating himself from the wilderness, Tayo has committed a sinful act, and until the guilt from that act can be expiated through reclaiming a sacred relationship with the captive land, Tayo and his community will also remain captives.

But Silko's *Ceremony* is not simply a reversal of the Anglo myth system, nor does it merely replace the Anglo version with an Indian one. Both Anglo and Indian captivity narratives traditionally sought the restoration of cultural and racial purity and the reaffirmation of proper borders through the redemption and return of the captive. The successful restoration of the captive mimed the restoration of the community to a previous state of spiritual wholeness and fidelity, reenforcing the boundaries safely separating the community from the dangerous influence of its enemies.

Silko's new mythic narrative seeks the reverse. She invokes cultural and racial hybridity, violated borders, a kind of spiritual polygamy. There is no hoped-for return to a pre-Columbian past before the arrival of whites when Indian peoples had an imagined purity of religious practices, cultural values, or social identities. Silko readily accepts and integrates objects and ideas from non-Indian and non-Pueblo worlds. She seeks a sacred marriage across rather than within the bounds of culture. The new mythic vision she creates is more than racially hybridized—it is spiritually and culturally mixed as well, a decolonizing myth allowing the subaltern group to subvert imperialism from within modern history, rather than reverting to a futile attempt to avoid it by returning to a pre-conquest past.

This hybridization is indicated early on through her choice of hero. Tayo is only half Indian. His father is unknown, either white or Mexican, and Tayo has been ridiculed all his life by other Indians for having light skin and "mexican" eyes.[5] His entire existence, in fact, is a sign of shame to his community, a constant signifier of its own impurity, pollution, and violated borders. Karen Wallace claims that in *Ceremony,* "the mixed-blood protagonists are . . . split between cultures and . . . are unable to maintain any enduring sense of self. The ultimate solution . . . comes to be an acknowledgment of tradition. . . . Each character's process depends on the conscious assimilation of those elements in himself that are . . . 'American' through a native framework" (96). I would argue, however, that Silko deliberately deconstructs the idea of the existence of an untainted "native" framework.[6] Rather than assimilation or "nativization," she advocates hybridization.

Silko invokes racial and cultural impurity as strength rather than weakness in several ways, most obviously through the bodies of the spotted cattle. These cattle are Josiah's answer to the white scientists' assumption of the superiority of their racially pure herefords. Josiah's spotted cattle, a hybrid of Anglo herefords and Mexican longhorns, look nothing like the diagram of the ideal beef cow in the breeding books. The Mexican longhorns are lean, tough and semi-wild, able to withstand droughts and blizzards and live on nothing but cactus and sagebrush. The Herefords, on the other hand, though providing much more beef, are too stupid to even look for water on their own, and if a windmill breaks down or a pool goes dry, they will simply stand and wait for someone to bring them water. Tayo recalls that if "nobody came and there was no snow or rain, then they died there, still waiting" (79). The spotted cattle, however, their mixed natures signified even in the patterns of their hides, are neither as skinny as the Mexican cows nor as stupid as the herefords. They are the physical embodiment of the best of both worlds, mythic signifiers of the hybridized, impure identities that are the inevitable, albeit unintended, consequence of conquest and imperialism.

The quest to redeem these hybrid cattle from their captivity at the hands of the white rancher who has stolen them is a major part of the overall ceremony that will redeem and restore Tayo himself. He is guided in this and other ceremonial aspects by an equally mixed group of individuals. The first of the series of ceremonies Silko shows the reader is the attempt by a Pueblo holy man, Ku'oosh, to restore Tayo with the traditional Pueblo ritual of the Scalp Ceremony. This ritual, unchanged through hundreds of years, is meant to purify warriors returned from battle who have become polluted through contact with an enemy and is performed for other returning World War II veterans, as well.

It fails for several reasons. Like the herefords or the longhorns, the "pure" rituals can address only part of the current realities of the postmodern world. As a mixed-blood person, a living symbol of the colonized state of their culture, Tayo has not been initiated into the religious world of the clans as a "pure" Laguna boy would have been. The power of rituals from that world can only partially redeem him, since as a despised half-breed in his own community, he has no place of original purity to which he might be restored. Ku'oosh, on the other hand, has not been initiated into the realities of the world outside the reservation or the experiences that have caused Tayo's sickness and captivity. Tayo reflects that "the old man would not have believed white warfare. . . . It was all too alien to comprehend . . . and even if he could have taken the old man to see the target areas, even if he could have led him through the fallen jungle trees and muddy craters of torn earth to show him the dead, the old man would not have believed anything so monstrous" (36–37).

Ku'oosh recognizes that the old rituals no longer function in the modern world but does not understand how the situation may be remedied. He tells Tayo sadly, "There are some things we can't cure like we used to . . . not since the white people came. The others who had the Scalp Ceremony, some of them are not better either. . . . I'm afraid of what will happen to all of us if you and the others don't get well" (38). In a mixed, hybridized, and impure world, the purely traditional ceremony from a now-vanished past can do no more than offer some temporary relief.

This is not the first ceremony Tayo has encountered, however. Before he even leaves for the Philippines he has a strangely ritualized encounter with a Mexican cantina dancer known as Nightswan who lives above a bar in the town of Cubero, on the outskirts of the Laguna reservation. In the traditional Pueblo world, she is a dangerous outsider, scorned by most of the Indians and the cause of much shame when Tayo's uncle Josiah begins an affair with her. It is she, however, who provides Josiah with the spotted cattle, and she is the first example in the novel of the hybridized spiritual world Silko invokes.

Nightswan is a living symbol of the feminine power of nature, a semi-mythical figure who once used the power of her dancing to dance a man to death. She left the town of Soccorro, where that incident occurred, and rode the bus until, she says, "'I saw the mountain, and I liked the view from here.' She nodded in the direction of the mountain Tse-pi'na, the woman veiled in clouds" (87). Though she is not an Indian, and not a version of any traditional Pueblo mythical figure, Silko ties her to the sacred site of Mount Taylor (Tse-pi'na), most obviously through the continued mention of the color blue, constantly associated in the novel with Mount Taylor. Nightswan lives in a room with blue walls, wears blue slippers and a blue kimono, even has blue sheets on her bed, blue-painted clay cups, and a bright blue door. Kathleen Manley notes that blue has special significance in both Pueblo and Hispanic cultures. For the Pueblos, she writes, blue is associated with daylight, dawn, and femaleness; for many Hispanics it is tied to the Virgin Mary and protection against witches (134). Mount Taylor is often described in the novel as appearing blue, and indeed Nightswan's association with the site is so strong, according to Robert Nelson, "It is as though Nightswan's destination has always been Mount Taylor, as though that is what she has been becoming, as well as where she has been going" (287).

Tayo finds her in her blue room surrounded by symbols of living nature: the smell of rain and wet earth, the sound of cottonwood leaves, and her perfume, which smells like "ivory locust blossoms" (97). By engaging in ritualized lovemaking with her in the midst of a life-giving rainstorm, Tayo is initiated into a spiritual world that is both a part of the traditional sacred mysteries of Grandmother Spider's world and at the same time something much larger. Silko makes clear that in this new mythic narrative, holiness has nothing to do with ethnicity or even one particular religion. In other words, even though she is Mexican and viewed with suspicion and even hatred by most of the Laguna, Nightswan is clearly in the service of the sacred and can be seen as an avatar, or physical embodiment, of the sacred power of nature.

As Tayo prepares to leave her rooms, she tells him she has been watching him for a long time, even though this is the first time Tayo has met her. She tells him he was marked for her by his "mexican" eyes, the sign of his impurity. When Tayo recalls with bitterness how the other children teased him because of his eyes, Nightswan tells him, "They are afraid, Tayo. They feel something happening, . . . and it scares them. Indians or Mexicans or whites—most people are afraid of change. They think that if their children have the same color of skin, the same color of eyes, then nothing is changing. . . . They are fools. They blame us, the ones who look different. That way they don't have to think about what has happened inside themselves. . . . You don't have to understand what is happening. But remember this day. You will recognize it later. You are part of it now" (99–100).

What Tayo is part of is a much larger ceremony, encompassing whites, Indians, Mexicans, and, as he later comes to realize, Japanese, Filipinos, and in fact all humans—the ultimate hybridization ritual.

If Nightswan symbolizes the mixed nature of the spiritual world, the mixed ceremonies of Silko's captivity myth are best embodied by Betonie, the Navajo holy man to whom Tayo's uncle Robert sends him in a last-ditch effort at restoration. This is itself contrary to the usual trajectory of captivity narratives, as the Navajo and Pueblo peoples are traditional enemies. Tayo even wonders briefly if Robert has not delivered him into another form of captivity in order to get rid of him, speculating that Betonie plans to murder him and dump his body as soon as Robert leaves.

While Tayo has no particular hatred of Navajos, even he is disturbed by the signs of mixture and impurity he sees at Betonie's hogan and in his speech and actions. When the old man speaks to him in perfect English and laughs at his surprise, "Tayo could feel the tiny hairs along his spine spring up. This Betonie didn't talk the way Tayo expected a medicine man to talk. He didn't act like a medicine man at all" (118). Tayo is so frightened by his unorthodox behavior he considers running away and the old man tells him, "Go ahead . . . . Most of the Navajos feel the same way about me. You won't be the first one to run away" (118). Like Tayo, Betonie is also of mixed blood with telltale hazel eyes. His grandmother, he tells Tayo, was a Mexican taken captive by Navajos while just a young girl, but as the daughter of a Mexican curandera, she was already a part of the ceremony that Tayo begins to realize not only encompasses himself, the Pueblos, and the Navajos but stretches across the oceans and across time. Betonie's grandmother is a sort of anti-captive in this myth, frightening her Navajo captors so much they actually pay an old medicine man, Betonie's grandfather, to take the girl off their hands.

The idea of the power of cultural mixing as a redemptive source is first made apparent to Tayo inside Betonie's hogan. This traditional Navajo dwelling is filled with what Tayo recognizes as the traditional paraphernalia of a medicine man: painted gourd rattles, deer-hoof clackers, and skin pouches. But many of these items are stored in cardboard boxes and Woolworth shopping bags, stacked alongside scores of calendars, phonebooks, and newspapers from Phoenix and Albuquerque, dating back decades. "[Tayo] wanted to dismiss all of it as an old man's rubbish . . . but the boxes and trunks were plainly part of the pattern: they followed the concentric shadows of the room" (120).

Tayo can feel the ritual power in the hogan, though he cannot understand how objects from the white world could function in a Native American setting. Betonie explains, "In the old days it was simple. A medicine person could get along without all these things. But nowadays . . ." (121). The need to integrate objects from all cultures in rituals dealing with the world of the sacred was taught to Betonie by his Mexican grandmother, who sent him to school at the Sherman Institute in Riverside, California, insisting he learn English because, she explained, "It is carried on in all languages now" (121). And yet Betonie in no way rejects the power of traditional Indian knowledge or worldviews. When a single hair comes loose from his mustache, he carefully locks it away in a trunk in the back of his hogan, as protection against the machinations of witches.

Betonie explains to Tayo that to be effective in the mixed world brought about by the Anglo invasion and colonization, old ceremonies must be altered, a disturbing process that his grandfather had begun many years ago. The old Navajo medicine man who had redeemed the young Mexican girl from her captors in order to help him carry on the great ceremony "flexed the old chants and beliefs like a mountain-oak bow" (150), and Betonie tells Tayo that just as in his grandmother and grandfather's day,

> The people nowadays have an idea about the ceremonies. They think the ceremonies must be performed exactly as they have always been done. . . . But long ago when the people were given these ceremonies, the changing began, if only in the aging of the yellow gourd rattle or the shrinking of the skin around the eagle's claw. . . . You see in many ways, the ceremonies have always been changing. . . . At one time the

ceremonies as they had been performed were enough for the way the world was then. But after the white people came, elements in this world began to shift; and it became necessary to create new ceremonies. I have made changes in the rituals. The people mistrust this greatly, but only this growth keeps the ceremonies strong.

She taught me this above all else: things which don't shift and grow are dead things. (126)

Tayo's epiphany at this moment marks a turning point in the narrative, and serves to illuminate Silko's vision of mythic change. The reason for the failure of the traditional Scalp Ceremonies is made clear to Tayo, as well as the reason for the failure of the VA doctors to cure him. Neither the rigid orthodoxy of the Pueblo medicine men nor the equally rigid orthodoxy of the white doctors and schoolteachers can fully encompass the physical and spiritual realities of the postmodern world. Tayo recalls that the white doctors at the VA hospital had yelled at him that he must forget about the others and think only of himself or he would not get well. "But he had known the answer all along. . . . medicine didn't work that way, because the world didn't work that way. His sickness was only part of something larger, and his cure would be found only in something great and inclusive of everything" (125–26). For Silko this is the new, mythic story she tells and the mixed ceremony that makes it possible. The community to which Tayo must be restored is no longer simply Laguna Pueblo, and his captivity is not simply at the hands of whites, as Betonie tells him: "Nothing is that simple. . . . you don't write off all the white people just like you don't trust all the Indians" (128). Even Tayo's seemingly inexplicable hallucination of Josiah standing among the Japanese POW's awaiting execution on a Philippine battlefield is now made clear, as Betonie explains that Tayo was simply seeing who the Japanese were, that "thirty thousand years ago, they were not strangers" (124), making an oddly circular connection between the postmodern and the prehistoric.

Wallace, like many critics, has read Betonie and the other mixed-blood characters in the novel as liminal figures, writing that Betonie "successfully negotiates the margins of cultures, maintaining a position in each through his liminal status" (99). But what Silko has done here is to create a new center. Neither Betonie nor Tayo function as marginal beings; rather they stand at the point where multiple cultures overlap and finally become focused, like the convergence of the disparate views through the two lenses of a pair of binoculars, which only achieve three-dimensionality upon crossing in a newly focused middle.

Betonie guides Tayo through a series of smaller rituals forming part of the great ceremony and like Silko's new myth, constructed out of the pieces of the old from multiple cultures. The Bear Ceremony Betonie enacts with Tayo above the junkyards of Gallup is one instance of Silko's modification of a traditional ceremony, this one of Navajo origin. Both its traditional and modern purpose is to redeem a member of the community who has become lost. Sometimes this captivity is through the malicious acts of coyote or an evil witch, sometimes simply through human bumbling, as when a small child wanders off from his parents,

When they tracked him the next day
his tracks went into the canyon
near the place which belonged
to the bears. They went
as far as they could
to the place
where no human
could go beyond,
and his little footprints
were mixed in with bear tracks.

So they sent word for this medicine man
to come. He knew how
to call the child back again. (129)

The bears have kindly taken in the lost child and raise him as their own. Nonetheless, he is human and needs to be redeemed to his proper relatives through a ritual narrative reenactment of his disappearance and a ceremony that will gently guide him to reintegration with his community. This ceremony, which Betonie uses to remind Tayo of at least one aspect of his identity, is similar to the actions of many white captives who would ritually repeat Bible verses or bits of remembered sermons to remind themselves not to lose their "true" identities by succumbing to the lure of their captor's culture.

But it is the figure of Ts'eh who is perhaps the most emblematic of Silko's postmodern synthesis of old and new, of a mythic vision grown from many cultures into something larger than any one. Robert Nelson writes "she should probably be taken as the mountain avatar of the genetrix spirit—a version of Tse pi'na, 'the woman veiled in clouds,' as well as a more youthful version of the Night Swan" (292). I believe, however, that Silko intends her to be, in effect, the avatar of the earth itself, the female representative of the nature goddesses from all cultures.

She appears to Tayo in the form of a very traditionally dressed Pueblo woman but possesses a Navajo blanket with a storm pattern woven into it with which she is able to control the elements. She lives on Mt. Taylor, the sacred mountain Tse-pi'na (her name, Ts'eh, being a shortened version of that word), and when Tayo asks her family name, she replies, "I'm a Montaño" (223), a Spanish word meaning mountain. She tells Tayo she has many brothers and sisters and insinuates that he has heard all about her "family" though Tayo, still thinking prosaically, cannot recall meeting anyone bearing that name. She further demonstrates that her sacred nature reaches beyond Mt. Taylor and Laguna culture by stating that her family is not only large but encompasses everything she and Tayo can see from where they stand, a high mesa on top of Mt. Taylor where it seems to Tayo "as if he had stepped from the earth into the sky; where they were, the sky was more than half the world" (223). She gestures over the immensity spread below them, saying she has a "sister" married to a Navajo from Red Lake, another near Flagstaff, and one in Jemez.

In other words, her spirit siblings live not just in a place sacred to the people of Laguna Pueblo but over all the earth. In addition, the brother/husband/hunter who lives with her in her remote mountain cabin first appears to Tayo with a newly killed deer over his shoulder, singing a traditional Laguna hunting song. He switches easily, however, into another song from Zuni and then into a third song whose origins Tayo cannot identify at all. Tayo marvels at his linguistic dexterity, wondering where he could have learned such a range of traditional songs. Like Ts'eh, he is a spirit representative, the sacred hunter from many cultures, not just Laguna. In a subversion of the expected presentation of these spiritual beings in a pure, pre-contact state, the hunter has killed his deer, not with a bow and arrow, but with a rifle he carries slung over one shoulder, Daniel Boone style. Ts'eh herself, as Tayo notes when he first encounters her, does not even have typical Indian features, but light skin and eyes, like Tayo's own.

The central ritual of the ceremonial restoration Tayo must complete in order to free himself from captivity is sexual union—first with Nightswan and then with Ts'eh. This is a form of the mythic sacred marriage so abhorred in Anglo captivity narratives. In completing this ritual with Ts'eh, as he had earlier with Nightswan, Tayo has enacted a sexual union with the body of nature. The first time Tayo and Ts'eh make love, Tayo likens his progress over her body to keeping track of trail markers and feels her body close around him "like river sand, softly giving way under foot, then closing firmly around the ankle in cloudy warm water. . . . When it came it was the edge of a steep riverbank crumbling under the downpour until suddenly it all broke loose" (181). Later, he falls asleep in a canyon beside a pool and dreams: "He felt the warm sand on his toes and knees; he felt her body, and it was as warm as the sand, and he couldn't feel where her body ended and the sand began" (222).

Ts'eh is essentially the spiritual embodiment of the earth itself—as Nightswan is the spirit of Mt. Taylor—and her task is the care of the earth and the maintenance of a balance in the natural world. She can be thought of as both Corn Woman and Reed Woman, even as Grandmother Spider or Thought Woman, but Silko has carefully delineated her as all of these in general and none of them in particular. By uniting himself with her in the mythic sacred marriage and assisting her in her duties, Tayo redeems himself from the guilt of having cursed the rain away in the Philippines and reconnects himself to the creative, spiritual power of the wilderness. As a member of a larger community, his restoration acts in part as the restoration of others, as well. Like the sacred hunters in the traditional European, Anglo American, and Native American myths, he acts not simply for himself but on behalf of his community.

The ceremonies of restoration alone, however, are not enough. To be fully redeemed, Tayo must also perform for his community the task of witch-finding. Like the old ceremonies Betonie has enlarged and expanded, the witches, representatives of evil in the world, have also moved beyond their traditional forms as recognized by the Indians. Silko gives several descriptions of them in the verse narratives, as though telling a traditional Pueblo tale, although the story she narrates is entirely of her own making. Many details are drawn from traditional Pueblo beliefs about witches, such as their obsession with bones, skins, and dead bodies. But Silko re-crafts these visions to suit her new myth, so the witches are from all tribes and races:

Some came from far far away
across oceans
across mountains.
Some had slanty eyes
others had black skin.
. . . they all got together
witch people from all directions
witches from all the Pueblos
and all the tribes. (133)

The multiethnic witches have a contest to see who can conjure the most evil, and the winner is a witch who "stood in the shadows beyond the fire/and no one ever knew where this witch came from/which tribe/or if it was a woman or a man" (134). The witch produces no profane or unholy objects but simply tells a story that, like the story Silko narrates as unfolding while Thought Woman thinks it, begins to happen as the witch tells it. This witch is spinning a new myth that is being reified in the course of its telling—literally creating the world, as all myths do, by compelling belief in itself and its narrative. The story is of the coming of white people who bring with them disease, starvation, and massacres, and for whom the natural world, the rocks, plants, and animals, are dead things. Like the witches themselves, the white people will use the dead things to create more evil:

> *Up here*
> *in these hills [near what is now Los Alamos Nuclear Laboratories]*
> *they will find the rocks,*
> *rocks with veins of green and yellow and black.*
> *They will lay the final pattern with these rocks*
> *they will lay it across the world*
> *and explode everything. (137)*

The witches are the antithesis of the figure of the sacred hunter, which Tayo has become in his hunt for the spotted cattle and his sacred marriage to the avatar of nature. They do not love what they hunt; they do not seek an exchange of identities nor a creative renewal of community. Rather, their aim is the destruction of life. In a world now united by imperialism, those in service to the witchery come in all colors and all races, and their evil crosses all boundaries of ethnicity and nation. Emo, a modern Indian witch, for example, does not use bobcat or wolf skins to generate evil but a bag of human teeth he collected in the Philippines from the corpses of Japanese soldiers. When Tayo wonders bitterly, "what good Indian ceremonies can do against the sickness which comes from their wars, their bombs, their lies?" (132), Betonie explains, "That is the trickery of the witchcraft. . . . They want us to believe all evil resides with white people. Then we will look no further to see what is really happening. They want us to separate ourselves from white people" (132). While such separation is the aim of most captivity narratives, Silko constructs separation and containment as the aim of evil and the goal of the witches. Betonie warns Tayo that the witches are a part of all communities, crossing racial, ethnic, and cultural boundaries. Now that Tayo is himself a semi-mythical figure, a participant in the great mythic ceremony, the witches will attempt to kill him to prevent him from completing the ceremony and restoring himself and his community.

Tayo's task then becomes one of identifying and defeating the witches operating within his world. The Puritan idea, like that of the East Coast Indians, was that the captive, having been in close contact with evil, is presumed to be able to recognize its forms, thereby allowing proper representatives of the community (Cotton Mather or other church fathers or those in the Medicine Society, for example) to drive out or execute witches polluting the communal body. In Puritan New England, the evil spirits guiding and inhabiting these witches often took the form of Indians, deer, or other inhabitants of the wilderness. In later Western works grown from the captivity narratives, the captive-turned-Indian-fighter becomes what Henry Nash Smith calls "the-man-who-knows-Indians." He combines the roles of identifier and executioner. Like the captive, he understands the Indians' ways, but more importantly, he is able to use his knowledge to defeat them militarily and drive them out, leaving the land cleansed and therefore safe for white habitation, in a sort of secular exorcism. In either case, however, compromise with the Indians is seen as impossible. The captivity myth, according to Slotkin, "allows only two responses to the Indian and to evil, either passive resignation or violent retribution in the name of a transcendent and inhuman justice" (141).

Silko reverses this dichotomy. Tayo engages in neither passive resignation nor violent retribution when he identifies the witches who are working to bring about his own death and the worldwide destruction promised by their acts at Trinity site and Los Alamos, nor does he succumb to a blind hatred of whites. Silko is able to subvert the paradigm of helpless victim or enraged killer so central to previous versions of the myth through Tayo's revelation about the changed nature of humanity—the largest communal body—and this new myth's deconstruction of borders and the identities they attempt to enforce.

Tayo hides in the rocks above the open pit of the mine from which the U.S. government obtained the uranium it would use to build the first atomic bomb. He is hiding from Emo, who intends to kill him and thus disrupt the ceremony that will redeem Tayo and restore his community. Tayo realizes it is no coincidence that this living myth-ceremony should be enacted at this precise spot in the modern American West at the site of the creation of the greatest modern evil:

> He had been so close to it, caught up in it for so long that its simplicity struck him deep inside his chest: Trinity Site, where they exploded the first atomic bomb, was only three hundred miles to the southeast, at White Sands. And the top-secret laboratories where the bomb had been created were deep in the Jemez Mountains, on land the Government took from Cochiti Pueblo: Los Alamos, only a hundred miles northeast of him now, still surrounded by high electric fences and the ponderosa pine and tawny sandrock of the Jemez mountain canyon where the shrine of the twin mountain lions had always been. There was no end to it; it knew no boundaries; and he had arrived at the point of convergence where the fate of all living things, and even the earth, had been laid. From the jungles of his dreaming he recognized why the Japanese voices had merged with Laguna voices, with Josiah's voice and Rocky's voice; the lines of cultures and worlds were drawn in flat dark lines on fine light sand, converging in the middle of witchery's final ceremonial sand painting. From that time on, human beings were one clan again, united by the fate the destroyers planned for all of them, for all living things; united by a circle of death that devoured people in cities twelve thousand miles away, victims who had never known these mesas, who had never seen the delicate colors of the rocks which boiled up their slaughter. (246)

The irony here is that the most deadly symbol of modern American imperialism, the ultimate product of the frontier myth, is the very thing that finally destroys the racial, national, and cultural borders it was intended to protect. Patricia Clark Smith and Paula Gunn Allen argue that Silko has made us see the American West as "the nexus of all modern history. . . . Tayo is not a single shell-shocked veteran suffering from flashbacks but a figure at the geographic and spiritual center of a cosmic illness" (191–92). Tayo's realization in the cosmic center of the American West that all people, all races, all cultures are one represents a profound change in the narrative trajectory of captivity myths, which have traditionally been constructed around the idea of separation and the mortal dangers of contact with the Other. Silko has perceived the dilemma inherent in the popular form of the myth. She reveals the tragic and ultimately destructive consequences implicit in the myth's insistence on violent retribution or passive acceptance of death as the only response to the threat of penetrated cultural or racial borders and moves her myth in an entirely different direction.

As Tayo crouches in the rocks, he watches Emo, Leroy, and Pinkie drive up to the sandy clearing below him and begin to torture Tayo's friend Harley in a deliberate attempt to force Tayo to fulfill the strictures of the captivity myth, to either submit to them or engage in some "violent retribution in the name of a transcendent and inhuman justice." Pinkie and Leroy, directed by Emo, cut off chunks of flesh from the screaming Harley, and Emo looks up into the rocks where he knows Tayo is hidden, yelling, "Look at this, you half-breed! White son of a bitch! You can't hide from this! Look! Your buddy, Harley" (252). Tayo has found a screwdriver earlier in the night, which he holds in one hand. He realizes the three torturers are very drunk. At one point Pinkey and Leroy begin fighting each other, and the drunken Emo momentarily turns his back on Tayo to watch them. Tayo "closed his fingers around the screwdriver and squeezed it until it was part of his hand. . . . He visualized the contours of Emo's skull; the GI haircut exposed thin bone at the temples, bone that would flex slightly before it gave way under the thrust of the steel edge. . . . This was the time. . . . There would be no one to help Emo" (252–53).

Tayo, in other words, is given ample justification for killing Emo. In fact, the typical captivity narrative functions, in part, to justify acts of violence by detailing the atrocities the innocent captive suffers at the hands of the savage Other. Besides passive acceptance of death, which would decree symbolically the death of the captive's community as well, the only alternative is violent retribution. The captor must be killed, both as punishment for transgressing the boundaries meant to protect the community from its enemies and to ensure that no future transgressions can occur. In killing Emo, then, Tayo would not only be justified in doing so in order to protect and revenge Harley (even though Tayo knows Harley has betrayed him to Emo), but he would be justified in killing a witch and thereby preventing future evils that might be committed by the witch. Killing Emo would seem right to audiences accustomed to the form of the captivity narrative and the outcome it demands.

Silko, however, has subverted this expectation by subverting the distinctions between captor and captive. If all people are one clan now, all members of one common human community, there is no pollution in mixing, no impurity in a crossed border, indeed no real borders to be penetrated or crossed. The need for separation and violent retribution, and a captivity myth to justify it, is negated. In fact, the traditional captivity narrative itself is now implicated as a source of evil and a product of witchery, with the Indian-fighter hero envisioned as a pawn of evil rather than a savior. Indeed, Tayo realizes that if he kills Emo, he will be doing exactly what the witchery wanted.

In this new vision, Tayo neither surrenders himself to Emo nor kills him. Instead, he rewrites the myth by dropping the screwdriver and moving back into the protective boulders where he waits for the sunrise. Harley, he reasons, will die either way, accepting, despite his sorrow at his friend's death, that "Harley had bargained for it; he realized that Harley knew how it would end if he failed to get the victim he had named" (252). Tayo understands also that this third, nonviolent course has successfully completed the ceremony and that any other action would have been to succumb to evil and to reaffirm the structure of the old myth: "It had been a close call. The witchery had almost ended the story according to its plan; Tayo had almost jammed the screwdriver into Emo's skull the way the witchery had wanted.... Their deadly ritual for the autumn solstice would have been completed by him" (253).

By subverting the expected outcome of the captivity narrative, Tayo as captive has been freed. His acceptance of the role of sacred hunter and participation in the sacred marriage has restored him to the community of nature. Tayo vows to continue Ts'eh's work, gathering the plants and seeds she has shown him and planting them in the proper places to ensure the rains. As a sign of the completion of the ceremony and the renewal of the relationship between people and the earth, Tayo sees as he leaves his hiding place "the clouds with round heavy bellies had gathered for the dawn. It was not necessary, but it was right, and even if the sky had been cloudless the end was the same" (255). As he staggers, exhausted, back toward the reservation, he dreams he sees his uncle Josiah, his grandmother, and Rocky wrapping him in a blanket and placing him in Josiah's old wagon. "Josiah was driving the wagon, old Grandma was holding him, and Rocky whispered 'my brother.' They were taking him home" (254).

Tayo is thus restored here to both the wilderness and his immediate family. Although the conventional formula of the captivity narrative concludes with the return and restoration of the captive, the feeling that the captive is still somehow marked—tainted and impure—often lingers, both in the mind of the captive and the community. Although the captive is returned, he or she may remain emotionally isolated from the community, having, as Slotkin notes "experienced a thing that his fellows have not, and his return to their presence is therefore not complete" (111). For Tayo, already partially outcast from his community because of his mixed ancestry, a return to purity is even more problematic.

Again, Silko has recognized the contradiction inherent in the traditional captivity myth: that once a border has been penetrated, there can be no return to purity, no final or complete separation. The mark of the Other can never be entirely erased. Captivity myths sought to address the anxiety generated by the subconscious acknowledgement of this reality without ever truly succeeding, but Silko has reversed the search for a restoration to purity for the captive and his or her community and replaced it with a search for impurity and hybridity.

Tayo, a sign and symbol of violated borders and mixed identities, is invited for the first time to enter the sacred kiva by the medicine man Ku'oosh upon his return. He spends an entire day telling Ku'oosh and the other elders his story, bringing the impure, hybridized world outside the reservation into the carefully preserved purity of the kiva and explaining the new shape of the myth as it now exists.

Like Betonie and his grandparents, Tayo brings change, but rather than making a futile attempt to cleanse Tayo of the marks of his difference, the elders accept his story and embrace him, initiating him into the sacred clan society. This could be read as an attempt to reject the impurity Tayo represents by containing it safely within the traditional bounds of the kiva clan societies, but I would argue that just as Betonie utilized both traditional and nontraditional items in his ceremonies, by portraying the elders as listening closely to Tayo's story and rejoicing at the outcome of the mixed and hybridized ceremony he completed, Silko is suggesting that change, even within the conservative world of the kiva societies, has begun. A. LaVonne Brown Ruoff agrees, stating that for Silko, "the strength of tribal traditions is based not on American Indians' rigid adherence to given ceremonies or customs but rather on their ability to adapt traditions to ever-changing circumstances by incorporating new elements" (167).

Silko's new mythic archetype then, is both typically Western and startlingly unorthodox, a story grown from the experience of colonization and from a Western narrative form stretching back at least three hundred years, crossed with and altered by Pueblo traditions reaching back even further. She has carried this mix and the bounds of the captivity myth itself forward into something profoundly different, offering an altered vision of a decolonizing subject and a new story for how America might begin to live with itself and its history.

CHAPTER 5

Sanctioned Narratives and the (Non)Innocent Triumph of the Savage War

Mythic Co-Dependence in Leslie Marmon Silko's *Almanac of the Dead*

> *Every society and official tradition defends itself against interferences with its sanctioned narratives, over time these acquire an almost theological status, with founding heroes, cherished ideas and values, national allegories having an inestimable effect in cultural and political life. . . . Paradoxically, the United States, as an immigrant society composed of many cultures, has a public discourse more policed, more anxious to depict the country as free from taint, more unified around one iron-clad major narrative of innocent triumph.*
>
> EDWARD SAID

In *Almanac of the Dead,* Leslie Marmon Silko attacks and disrupts the sanctioned narratives of American innocence and the presumption of the inevitable triumph of superior Anglo culture over the dark-skinned natives of the "New World" by subverting the most common vehicle of that mythic narrative, the Western. She challenges the mythical status of America's founding heroes and the "cherished ideas and values" that support them. Nonetheless, she depends upon the very myths she challenges. The result is a complex text, at once recognizably a Western and, simultaneously, radically opposed to the narratives of innocence most Westerns present. It is a work anchored in the myths of both Anglo and Indian cultures and one that demonstrates the dialogic interconnections between them, without ever entirely escaping their confines. She succeeds, however, in calling into question many of the most common assumptions about frontiers, borders, and their roles in constructing national(ist) identities for Americans and for those who fall under the shadow of American imperialism.

Almanac presents another, darker version of the decolonizing process Silko explores in *Ceremony.* Here she illustrates the modern process of mythogenesis in its most vicious form: building and destroying the identities of colonizer and colonized alike. The Mexican American border comes to hold special meaning as a signifier of the history of invasion and conquest that created it and the mythically directed acts of imperialism needed to uphold it. Ironically, however, the border is a symbol both of the power and the futility of imperialism. In a sense it structures the entire novel and directly or indirectly shapes the lives of every character in it. Individuals are defined as legitimate or alien depending on their position relative to it. The value of goods, both legal and illegal, increases or decreases as those goods are moved from one side of it to the other. Governments are ready, even eager, to kill in order to defend it. And yet, like the frontier, everywhere but nowhere in the mythic cyberspace of the twenty-first century, the border is maddeningly elusive. Dangerous, fluid, permeable, it is a product and producer of a particular brand of myth, structured, as in McCarthy's vision, around a privileged form of sacred violence all sides battle to claim for their own. The competing versions of myth generated to either uphold or erase this border and to legitimate the violence necessary for both or either action are astonishingly similar: hybridized, mixed, and frankly dependent upon each other for their very existence.

The struggle to legitimate this violence sits at the heart of American identity. Richard Slotkin argues in *Regeneration through Violence* that the founding fathers of the United States were not those august men who gathered in Philadelphia to draft a nation. Rather, they were "the Indian fighters, traders, missionaries, explorers, and hunters who killed and were killed until they had mastered the wilderness; the settlers who came after, suffering hardship and Indian warfare for the sake of a sacred mission or a simple desire for land; and the Indians themselves, both as they were and as they appeared to the settlers, for whom they were the special demonic personification of the American wilderness. Their concerns, their hopes, their terrors, their violence, and their justifications of themselves, as expressed in literature are the foundation stones of the mythology that informs our history" (4). Frontier sites, from which these foundation stones are dug, have entered the modern American imagination as the mythic birthplace of Anglo America, but they have also come to serve, through centuries of cultural imperialism, as a birthplace for non-Anglo America as well, with devastating consequences for both groups. The Mexican American borderlands, as the site of Anglo frontiers with both Indians and Mexicans, have become a sort of focal point of frontier images and mythogenesis. They can been seen as a place of convergence in the modern imagination from where Americans think about our various histories, our often contradictory myths, and the current issues troubling the nation—from bilingualism and race relations to environmental questions—that seem condensed and concentrated in this highly contested region.

The myths generated from and about the frontiers, though largely glorifying the deeds of white males and the "triumph" of white culture, are, nonetheless, the result of close contact and mixing between Anglo, Indian, and Mexican cultures. But while we may normally think about frontier myths as a source of power for Anglo culture, this idea is predicated on the assumption that Indian and Mexican cultures have died out, somehow disappeared from the United States under the triumphant onslaught of Anglo America, and no longer offer any real challenge to white hegemony. In a nation that is, in the words of Emma Pérez, caught in a time lag between the colonial and the postcolonial, a condition she terms the "decolonial imaginary," such assumptions must be scrutinized.[1]

Edward Said calls the continuing struggles between dominant and colonized cultures in the Americas and elsewhere "border wars" (311) and writes that whatever aims are attributed to such wars by dominant cultures, the effects are both impoverishing and essentializing, an attempt to force the subaltern Other to either give up his or her culture and join the dominant group or accept inferior status. Throughout the world, however, he notes that colonized cultures are frequently choosing a third alternative, one which by its very existence negates the sanctioned, theological narratives of an innocent and inevitable triumph already achieved by the founding fathers of the past. This choice is to fight, thereby challenging the notion of cultural or racial disappearance. Said cites the Palestinian intifada, the women's movement, and "various social, ecological and cultural movements throughout North and South America" (311) as examples of this resistance to sanctioned narratives. These movements today, he claims, "are developing, if not a general theory . . . then an underlying world map. Perhaps we may start to speak of this somewhat elusive oppositional mood, and its emerging strategies, as an internationalist counter-articulation" (311).

What Silko has done in *Almanac* is to present a counter-articulation of the mythologized story of white triumph in the Americas through the vehicle of the most common narrative form of that story. She does not write an Indian myth but deliberately combines elements of Indian culture and life throughout her story, emphasizing the mixed nature of both the colonizing and colonized cultures. The title of the novel refers to an ancient collection of writings originating with Mayan priests who survived the Spanish conquest and began recording their history and prophecies for the future.[2] The earliest parts of Silko's almanac are written on "thin sheets of membrane . . . primitive parchment the Europeans taught the native Americans to make" (246), ensuring that from the start, the text was hybridized and mixed by its very nature. Some writings appear in the form of Mayan glyphs, she says, but as the centuries progress and each keeper adds his or her own notes on the continuing history of the indigenous peoples of the Americas, the writing changes into Mayan transcribed phonetically by Indians who had learned classical Spanish, then into Spanish, then finally, as the notebooks make their way in the twentieth century to present-day Tucson, into English tapped out on a word processor. This hybridized and mixed text is woven throughout the novel, both contrasting and supporting the classic Western narrative of border wars and savage Others structuring the novel. Thus European technologies are seen as both destroying the Indian world that had previously existed in the Americas and paradoxically assuring its nondisappearance through the continued resistance of those who preserve the almanac and strive to bring into fruition the prophecies it provides.

As the almanac within the novel demonstrates, while no Indian culture in the Americas remains untouched by Anglo European culture, that is not to say that Indian cultures have simply become Anglo or unquestioningly accepted Anglo myths as their own, despite several hundred years of violent indoctrination. Any imagined purity that might have existed for precontact cultures is irrevocably gone. Native cultures today are borderlands cultures—mixed, hybridized, impure, indelibly marked by the culture of modern white America, even south of the border.

However, Anglo American culture is itself mixed and impure, bearing the mark of extended, often violent, contact with native Others, until even its own myths about itself are tangled and twined with myths from and about Indians. All sides here attempt to construct myths that will legitimize, cleanse, and shape the past and, through it, the present and the future, constantly reimagining what they were before the inevitable mixing that followed conquest and colonization. As Said points out, however, the striking consequence of such efforts in an imperial situation is never cultural purity but rather a vain attempt "to conceal how much the experience of the stronger party overlaps with and, strangely, depends on the weaker" (192).

One way the Anglo myth of the frontier has sought to veil this reality is by treating the borderlands as a former frontier now safely conquered, cleansed of the mark of the racialized Others that formerly inhabited it. Silko subverts this notion of safety and purity by constructing the border as the center of an ongoing battle that has never ceased, a site of decolonization violently opposed to the officially sanctioned narrative of innocent Anglo triumph put forward by the frontier myth structuring most Westerns. Both versions depend, however, on legitimization of the violence necessary to achieve their hoped-for visions.

This legitimized violence is what Slotkin, in *Gunfighter Nation,* calls the "savage war." He defines this type of warfare as both a mythic trope and an operative category of military doctrine, influencing American foreign policy and military operations from King Philip's War to Vietnam. The "savage war," he explains, is a special kind of warfare, one that comes about as the result of perceived ineluctable differences—racial, cultural, and social—that decree peaceful co-existence impossible and is accompanied and enabled by a specific sort of rhetoric. In a savage war with a barbarous enemy, the saying went, every fight was to the death, the enemy was completely without honor, and you always saved the last bullet for yourself. For Anglo Americans, then, the only relationship imaginable between whites and Indians became one of absolute extermination, a savage war with no possibility for compromise or honorable surrender by either side. In its most typical formulations, Slotkin writes "the myth of 'savage war' blames Native Americans as instigators. . . . The accusation is better understood as an act of psychological projection that made the Indians scapegoats for the morally troubling side of American expansion" (12–13). The insistence, then, that the other side would do the same to you if they had the chance helped white Americans justify the "morally troubling" realization that they often acted more savagely in their conquest of the continent than the so-called "savages" they castigated and displaced.

The trope of the savage war, tied to the national psyche with bonds of shame and justification, has also formed the ideological basis of the Western, from its birth as the captivity narrative to its evolution in the hands of Cooper, who recognized that the racial opposition between whites and Indians formed the ideological justification of American history, to modern Western novels and films that have made the image of the white cavalry riding to the rescue of innocent pioneers beset by painted savages ubiquitous to the point of (almost) comic cliché. Even our most stereotyped childhood game of make believe, "cowboys and indians," is a direct enactment of the savage war in miniature.

As a building block of the National Symbolic and one of our most familiar versions of National Fantasy, the savage war has become part of the American psyche but not only for white children. Acoma Pueblo writer Simon Ortíz tells of teaching elementary school on a reservation in Arizona and watching the children on the playground engaging in a game of "cowboys and indians," with the cowboys as the good guys and the Indians as the bad guys. He notes that he found in the children a curious sense of psychic dislocation.[3] When he questioned them about Indians as evil, the "enemy" in the "cowboys and indians" game, and the fact that they were themselves Indians, the children replied, "Oh, we're not *that* kind of Indian." "Well, what kind are you?" Ortíz asked. Some children named their tribe, some simply shrugged and said they didn't know, but all agreed that they weren't *that* kind of Indian.

That kind of Indian, however, is at the bedrock of the Western, the most common Other to be fought and overcome by the Anglo hero, more important in fact than the hero himself since American triumph in the savage war can remain innocent only if the enemy is savage beyond all redemption, thereby serving to highlight the wholesomeness of Anglo society and the rightness of its destruction of native peoples.[4] The trope of the triumph of civilization over savagery imagined in the frontier myth, with the Anglo hero slaying the bloodthirsty Indian warrior (often after rescuing a helpless white woman held captive by him) is the inescapable conclusion of the savage war.[5]

Just as Silko turned the traditional captivity narrative inside out in *Ceremony,* she now takes up the mythic trope of the savage war in *Almanac of the Dead* and twists it violently into something else—still distinctly a Western but a postmodern mythological work that transforms that genre into something entirely new. It is not a happy or innocent vision. All her characters, Anglo and Indian, black and white, are angry, bitter, and resentful, trapped within the deadly structure of the myth of Anglo triumph and the unquestioned necessity of savage warfare. Even those native characters who retain some knowledge of what Indian cultures were like before the arrival of Europeans view the struggle in which they are engaged through the lens of the Anglo myth of the savage war, with whites playing the part of the barbaric Others who must be eliminated at all costs.

The Western, with its underlying reliance on the savage war and concomitant assumption that Anglos have won it and slain their brown-skinned enemy, is predicated on the eventual disappearance of Indians. Jane Tompkins writes that while the presence of Indians in a work unquestioningly signals that one is in a Western, "Indians are repressed in Westerns—there but not there. . . . And when they do appear they are even more unreal" (9). This is because Indians are essentially dead in traditional Westerns, ghosts who may be evoked in historical flashback but who we all know will be defeated, even when they are portrayed sympathetically. Renee Bergland argues that portrayals of Indians as insubstantial spirits is common not only in Anglo American literature but in Native American works as well.[6] The portrayal of Indians as ghostly and uncanny, she argues, may allow them to haunt the national imagination, but it also keeps them safely dead, unable to directly affect the modern world. They have, she says, "vanished into the minds of those who have dispossessed them" (2). Even Silko, she claims, "ghosts" Indians in *Ceremony*, presenting Tayo as grey smoke at the outset of the novel, Rocky and Josiah as ghosts who haunt his dreams, and Ts'eh as a ghostly, spirit lover. Although she calls *Ceremony* a "creative subversion" (3) of the Anglo intent in ghosting Native Americans, she remains unconvinced that Silko truly presents an alternate vision of vanishing Indians.

I would argue, however, that ghosts play very different roles in Native American and Anglo American worldviews and thus in the literatures produced by each, mixed though those worlds may be. In the wake of Enlightenment, ghosts have been viewed by Europeans as figments of the imagination, psychic projections of repressed minds or guilty consciences. Not only insubstantial and disembodied but also not *real.* Native Americans are therefore doubly removed in Anglo American literature—doomed to defeat and death in the mythical savage war and reduced to a psychic metaphor of the white imagination in its aftermath. White Americans, in other words, don't really *believe* in ghosts or Indians. For Silko, that rational disbelief is precisely why Anglos will eventually lose the savage war they cannot admit they are still fighting.

Like any classic Western, *Almanac of the Dead* is centered on that war, filled with cowboys and Indians, ambushes and gunfights, outlaws, bandits, smugglers, and captives. But here we see the savage war as it is still carried out underground, in the interstices of the white world, at the end of the twentieth century. After five hundred years of warfare, the Americas in the 1990s are filled with ghosts Silko deliberately calls. These ghosts are indeed the projections of European guilt, but in the borderlands separating and joining Anglo, Indian, and Hispanic worlds, they are also *real.* The novel itself is their almanac, the record of their nondisappearance, the vehicle through which they can directly touch the modern world in their own "internationalist counter-articulations." Silko has claimed the Southwestern borderlands, a truly haunted place in the American imagination, and made it into a graveyard and birthplace, a battlefield where centuries of conquest and colonization, savage warfare and violent resistance spawn a mythic tale that presents a counter-version of the birth of one nation and the death of another and the consequences of the myths both sides choose to accept.

As the novel progresses, indigenous peoples from all parts of the Americas begin marching toward the Mexican American borderlands, some armed and some peacefully, but Silko suggests the mass movement will culminate in the final battle in the savage war as Indians from all tribes go "on the warpath," just as the myths and stories recorded in the ancient almanac predict. The ending Silko invokes, however, is not the inevitable disappearance and defeat of native peoples that underlie traditional Westerns but rather the final defeat and extermination of all things European in the Americas.

Her revisioned myth subverts many of the basic assumptions of the savage war in the Western but relies on many others, giving them a chilling and ironic twist by pushing the savage war unflinchingly into the twentieth century. The fact that few of her characters can envision any but a bloody and violent final meeting between Anglos and Indians is disturbing evidence of the power of sanctioned narratives to impose their worldviews, their versions of history and visions of the future, even on those peoples who resist them the most. Unlike Tayo in *Ceremony,* Silko's Indian characters in *Almanac* succumb willingly to the lure of righteous violence and a seemingly justified war, apparently unaware of the psychic dislocation that makes them act out an Anglo myth.

The historic West plays an important role in connecting the anger of modern Indians to the injustices of the past. The site of the final battle in the savage war is one commonly associated with Indian wars of past centuries: Tucson, Arizona. Built, Silko claims, on the blood money of arms and whiskey traders who willingly supplied both the U.S. Army and the Indians they fought, Tucson is the ugly, postmodern reality of the mythic "Wild West town" brought glaringly into the present without the rose-colored glasses of colonial nostalgia that so often shade such sites in traditional Westerns. Still run by smugglers, crooked politicians, corrupt sheriffs, and more or less lawfully armed bandits, rife with cheap saloons, whorehouses, sleazy motels, and drug dealers, Tucson is the antithesis of the longed-for outcome of the savage war in the Anglo vision.

Instead of a paradise successfully carved from the wilderness, free from the taint of the defeated savage Other, where white civilization thrives as proof of Anglo racial and cultural superiority, Tucson is hell on earth. While most of the surviving Indians have been reduced to abject poverty, they refuse to disappear. Along with poor Mexicans, they freely cross and re-cross the international border, ignoring both the U.S. and Mexican governments' insistence on their national sovereignty and security. They engage gleefully in smuggling drugs and archeological antiquities, so scarred by the effects of colonialism and poverty they reason that smuggling cocaine and looting their own archeological sites is acceptable because the people who will suffer the most from such actions are non-Indians. The governments of the invaders in Washington, D.C., and Mexico City are illegitimate, they point out, since "no legal government could be established on stolen land" (133). They are able to succeed as smugglers, traversing the deserts and mountains of the Southwestern borderlands with relative ease despite the damage drugs inflict on their own communities, because whites are even more devastated by their occupation of the stolen land than the Indians they have sought to erase.

The "New World" wilderness, like its native inhabitants, has also refused to "give up the ghost," so to speak, and submit quietly. It is a menacing and unknowable place to its European occupiers, as much a projection of their guilt and anxieties as the ghosts of their imaginations and just as unreal to them. The desert constantly threatens to overwhelm the whites who live there with searing heat and continuous drought, in seemingly deliberate defiance of Anglo technologies that allow for the drilling of mile-deep wells, massive irrigation projects, and artificial lakes meant to make the conquered wilderness bloom. Like the Indians themselves, once the land has been "ghosted" by Europeans, it becomes even less manageable, there but not there, both ubiquitous and invisible.

Tucson and its surrounding desert is not the new frontier in *Almanac*, nor is it simply the old frontier modernized for a present-day Western. Rather, Silko has altered the definition and purpose of frontiers and borderlands. Instead of functioning as the extreme, the outer edge, the far fringe of civilization, the Mexican American borderlands become the center, the place of convergence, the heart of the narrative viewpoint. While this region is also a site of violent conflict between Anglo, Indian, and Mexican cultures, Silko presents in overwhelming detail the reality of that conflict as present in all parts of the Americas. From the lake country of Canada, the alleys of New Orleans, the swamps of Florida, and the islands of the Caribbean, native tribes, Louisiana's Black Indians, and the descendents of rebel slaves of African and native blood continue to engage in violent resistance against their European colonizers, crossing racial and national borders to do so.

Before the main text of *Almanac* begins, Silko supplies the reader with a curious map of the Mexican American border region, presenting, as Said suggests, a subaltern Other's vision of geographic territory, "an underlying world map" speaking a counter-articulation of the dominant narrative. Silko labels her map "Almanac of the Dead: Five Hundred Year Map." Dividing the map into two equal halves is a straight horizontal line. Below the line is the word "MEXICO"; above it, dead center of the page, is Tucson. Dotted lines with tiny arrows originating from all corners of the map lead straight to Tucson like the spokes of a wheel, converging there from San Diego and El Paso, New Jersey and Chiapas, Haiti and Cuba. What is a distant frontier in the traditional narratives of the United States and Mexico, that which divides them from each other, becomes instead a central, burning line joining them together. The frontier as border is both affirmed and erased, its contrived and artificial nature scoffed at by its characterization as a perfectly and artificially straight line on the map and by the native characters in the book, who claim "the white man had always been trying to 'control' the border when no such thing existed to control except in the white man's mind" (592).

For the white characters, this incorporeal border is far more real than the ghosts and ancestor spirits the native characters acknowledge or even the living Indians themselves. With a growing influx of "illegal" immigrants crossing this ghostly line in the wake of indigenous uprisings and political turmoil in Mexico, the U.S. government decides to make Tucson "command headquarters for all U.S. military forces assembled along the Mexican border" (656), as the Mexican government is doing in the south. To both the Mexican and U.S. administrations, this defense of a national border seems logical, but for the millions of native peoples in the Americas answering dreams sent by native spirits and ancestor ghosts that command them to move along the ancient roads that have traditionally carried them north and south, the actions of the governments are ridiculous. By the last half of the novel, there is an army of Indians marching north from southern Mexico and another army of Mohawks and Lakotas marching south from Canada, picking up U.S. Indians along the way. What then will the border guards and army units do, Silko wonders? Will the Mexicans shoot north at the descending northern tribes, while American soldiers fire south at the Mayans and Yaquis? Or will each side turn its guns on its own citizens? Indians have managed to "ghost" the border here, turning it into an insubstantial projection of imperialist fantasy.

The governments of both nations are terrified of these Indian armies marching toward the border/heartland but oddly blind to them. They cannot see the rationale behind the movements and cannot understand who is leading such diverse tribes. It is, in fact, the rational, logical Anglo disbelief in the presence of spirits that shields the marchers, because these living armies are led and inspired by ghosts. Not the faded, disembodied shades of European imagination, however, but powerful spirits communicating with thousands through dreams and visions. Even seen through the eyes of Sterling, the Pueblo Indian who witnesses much of the modern signs of the coming last battle, they are terrifying: "Marching through his brain day and night were Lecha's 'armies' of Lakota and Mohawks; Sterling saw them over and over in dreams; ghost armies of Lakota warriors; ghost armies of the Americas leading armies of living warriors, armies of indigenous people to retake the land" (762). Coming from the south is an even larger army led by twin Mayan brothers, a modern version of the common trope of hero twins found in native myths in both North and South America. One of them is guided by the visions he receives from sacred macaws who transmit the voices of spirits and ancestor ghosts. In an ironic twist on the racist fears of the savage war reflected in cold war paranoia and rhetoric about communist takeovers, the other brother has been trained in military tactics by a Cuban communist agent. When this brother and his militaristic Indian lover, Angelita La Escapia (little angel, the meathook), feel they have learned all they can from "the Cuban" and tire of his Eurocentric blindness to native concerns and the voices of native spirits (no different, the brother thinks, from the equally blind capitalist Americans), they kill the Cuban as a message to the communists after a trial that turns his own rhetoric against him.

As an almanac, a document designed to predict, warn, and advise its readers about the future, Silko's *Almanac*, as many critics and even local Tucson news stations have pointed out, has proved thus far uncannily accurate. Published in 1992, its armed uprising by Mexican Indians from the southern state of Chiapas seemed to predict the January 1, 1994, armed uprising of Mexican Indians from Chiapas calling themselves the Zapatista National Liberation Army, and the army of Mohawks and Lakotas marching from Canada echoed the armed Mohawk confrontation with Canadian police and military forces in 1990 over expansion of a civic golf course into a tribal burial ground, an incident that resulted in increased political organizing among northern tribes. The Border Patrol in southern Arizona is today the largest and most heavily armed branch of that entity, frequently assisted by the U.S. military. Even the Zapatista spokesman, known as "subcomandante Marcos," echoes Silko's vision of a native world filled with violent and angry ghosts, announcing to the world press at the start of the uprising, "Here we are, the dead of all times, dying once again, but now with the objective of living."

The only characters in *Almanac* who can hear the dead, the ancestor ghost/spirits, are those who have native blood or those few Anglos who have rejected the world built by European rule in the Americas. Among these is the white leader of the Army of the Homeless and the healers at the Holistic Healers Convention held in Tucson where native participants "planned to take thousands of white 'converts' to aid and protect the twin brothers and their followers" (733). Most Anglos in the novel do not receive the dreams and visions sent by the ghosts and spirits, because, according to Silko, they left their own ancestor spirits behind in Europe and now, in the logical and rational twentieth century, willfully refuse to see or acknowledge those in the Americas.

Their rational disbelief in ghosts and spirits blinds them to other, more concrete realities as well, especially the realities of the land that they now occupy and the indigenous inhabitants who live on it. Calabazas, a Yaqui, recalls the elders of his village in Mexico explaining that "Europeans suffered a sort of blindness to the world. To them, a 'rock' was just a 'rock' wherever they found it, despite obvious differences in shape, density, color, or the position of the rock relative to all things around it. The Europeans, whether they spoke Spanish or English, could often be heard complaining in frightened tones that the hills and canyons all looked the same to them" (224–25). Silko deliberately highlights here the difference between living on a land and living with it. In other words, she presents as fantasy the common theme in Westerns regarding the Anglo hero's conquest and taming of the wilderness. Here Anglos may politically control the land and devastate it with strip mines, clear cutting, and toxic waste, but they cannot see it, do not really know it, and are therefore deaf and blind to the spirits (and Indians) that inhabit it.

As in traditional Westerns, however, Silko ties native people to the wilderness in a close relationship Europeans can only look at with envy or disdain. As a rock is just a rock to them, an Indian is just an Indian—disembodied, not quite real—in effect, already dead and, therefore, to the European mind, non-existent. Silko links the idea of Anglo blindness and the power of Indian spirits together with a series of stories about that most famous of savage Indians in the Anglo imagination: Geronimo. The first Geronimo story in the novel, told by Yoeme, grandmother of the twins Lecha and Zeta, who will carry the Almanac to the United States, claims that the man called Geronimo imprisoned in Oklahoma was an imposter who agreed to imprisonment so the real Geronimo could remain free to continue his work. Lecha unthinkingly records this story in the almanac in the language in which she is most comfortable; thus it becomes the first entry written in English, the sign, Yoeme reveals "the keepers of the notebooks had always prayed for" (130). Further Geronimo stories, not written in the almanac, follow. One claims Geronimo had been tricked into capture under a flag of truce, the only way white soldiers would ever have been able to catch him in the rugged deserts and mountains that seemed to protect and hide his band (221); another version is that an elderly Apache named Old Pancakes surrendered and claimed to be Geronimo, either as a joke or to protect the real Geronimo. White army officers, desperate to prove to the American public they could keep the Indians under control, were more than willing to believe him even after he recanted his story (229–30). Yet another version states that there were actually four different Apache warriors known as Geronimo living in the Arizona and New Mexico territories, one named "Red Clay, the final Geronimo who died in Oklahoma" (226), another called Sleet, the youngest of the Geronimos, who escaped to Mexico, a third named Big Pine, who had been arrested in a camp west of Tucson, and a fourth known to the Yaquis as Wide Ledge (224–25).

All these stories, told by native characters, agree, however, that the various photos still in existence of the man whites called Geronimo do not actually reflect the images of any of the men hunted, arrested, or photographed by the U.S. and Mexican armies. Rather, a long-dead ancestor, in order to protect the men and to enable them to do the work they had to do for their people on this earth, cast his image through the lens of the white men's cameras and caused his own likeness to appear in all the photographs, thus confusing the whites even further.

The validity of this ghostly explanation is never doubted by native characters and presented as real in the novel. As other critics have noted, Silko's work often contains elements of magical realism. As if to prove to modern readers that the old-time Indians were correct in their assessment of the ability of ancestors, spirits, and ghosts to magically influence Anglo technology, Silko presents the episode of the Eskimo woman and the weasel pelt, which takes place in the 1970s.

In this scene, which comes quite early in the novel, Lecha, one of the Mexican Indian twins who carries the almanac to Tucson, is spending the winter in a Yupik Eskimo village in Alaska near the Bering Sea after a failed affair with a dogsled racer. In the community meeting hall, her Eskimo friend Rose introduces her to an elderly Yupik woman rumored to be a witch. Sensing Lecha's destiny as a keeper of the ancient almanac, the old woman offers to demonstrate for her what she calls her "plane-crashing spell" (156). She rubs a special piece of weasel pelt against the screen of the community center's television, generating static electricity until the picture on the screen begins to swirl. “Then the old woman had closed her eyes and summoned all the energy, all the force of the spirit beings furious and vengeful” (157). She summons the ancestor spirits through recitations of stories of injustices committed against the Yupik people, “stories that were also indictments of the greedy destroyers of the land” (156). As Lecha watches, the weather channel map that had previously appeared on the screen changes into an image of a big river flowing into the sea and a fog bank that rushes up to engulf a plane whose engines can be heard laboring then fading before the screen goes completely white. The next day, Lecha hears of a plane crash, another in a series of unexplained crashes including that of the real-life Korean jet liner that drifted mysteriously off course before being shot down by the Soviet Union, just a few miles north of the village. According to Rose, “White people could fly circling objects [communication satellites] in the sky that sent messages and images of nightmares and dreams, but the old woman knew how to turn the destruction back on its senders” (156).

Much of the novel, in fact, resembles the old woman’s plane-crashing spell: a Western turned back upon its creators, a recitation of centuries of rape, theft, slavery, and genocide by whites against the Indian populations of the Americas. It could be argued that the intent is the same, as well. According to Jane Tompkins, this is the underlying intent of all Westerns, “the legitimization of physical violence” (174), and it is evident that most of Silko’s native characters in *Almanac* feel justified in engaging in any act of violence as long as it is directed against Anglos.

Perhaps the most disturbing aspect of the plane-crashing story is that none of the people involved, neither Lecha, Rose, nor the unnamed Yupik woman, are at all concerned over the loss of innocent lives in these crashes, not even for the planeload of Koreans who arguably had no connection at all to the conquest and exploitation of the Americas. In a tragic self-fulfilling prophecy, the Anglos’ five-hundred-year savage war against the Indians has left them as brutal and bloodthirsty as the Anglo myth imagined them to be. It has in fact left them, like whites, unquestioningly certain that the only possible outcome of the meeting between whites and Indians in the Americas is exactly what the Anglos claimed it must be—a savage fight to the death against a racial Other completely dehumanized in the eyes of their enemies. All non-Indians in the novel are greedy, selfish, and destructive, many obsessed with torture, death, or sexual perversions. But native characters are scarcely better. Other than the helpless and bumbling Sterling, who does little more than witness as various events unfold around him, the only vaguely sympathetic character in the novel is the white woman Seese, a former prostitute and drug addict whose baby has been kidnapped from her apartment as she lay in an alcohol- and drug-induced stupor. Lecha, who possesses the psychic ability to find missing persons, recruits the desperate Seese to aid her in typing up the disorganized pages of the almanac, promising to help Seese find her baby as soon as the work is completed, all the while deliberately withholding from her the truth that her baby is already dead.

In *Almanac*, then, we find the myth of innocent triumph that underlies the frontier myth stripped of its innocence. Typically, Westerns seem hopeful because their violence seems justified and therefore innocent. Their implicit promise of the new Eden that will come into being once the wilderness has been made safe for white settlement is rarely challenged with the brutal realities of the modern world that actually resulted from the savage war waged to create it. Like the ghosts of Indians murdered for the sake of white greed, however, the past remains to haunt the present in *Almanac*. The frontier myths created to justify European acts in the Americas, "the foundation stones of the mythology that informs our history," as Slotkin says, are turned back upon their makers, just as the old Yupik woman turns the evil dreams of the Anglo satellites back upon their senders. The result, however justified it may seem based upon Anglo history in the New World, is still, and inevitably, more and more bloodshed, a seemingly never-ending savage war.

Janet St. Clair argues that, despite portraying a "nightmarish wasteland of violence, bestiality, cruelty, and crime" (141), "the novel is by no means without hope" (151). She states that some characters, like the white man, Roy, who is organizing the Army of the Homeless, and the Barefoot Hopi, who goes to the Holistic Healers Convention to recruit white converts, invoke "anxious and concerned people of all colors to come together" (153) in order to achieve the "reclamation and restoration of loving relationships among people" (155). This seems to be an overly optimistic interpretation, however. Roy's army pledges to "burn down the city, take a police bullet, and die quick, because that way they died fighting" (748), while the Barefoot Hopi, who has recently been released from prison, where he was incarcerated for shooting down a helicopter full of tourists hovering over a Snake Dance at old Oraibi, dreams of the day when "prisons and jails all over the U.S. were hit with riots" (618), which he hopes will spread to every major city in an orgy of bloodshed and violence. The fact that many of the homeless are white, and that the Barefoot Hopi believes the rioters will be the poor and oppressed of all colors, seems a rather strained justification, no more innocent than the Anglo myths and equally unlikely to result in a new Eden whose society is structured by "loving relationships among people."

Silko does not entirely blame Anglos for this state of affairs, however. "Blood and its power had been misused by sorcerers," she writes; "Long before Europeans ever appeared, the people had already disagreed over the blood and the killing" (336). Montezuma and Cortéz, she claims, recognized each other immediately as fellow cannibals obsessed with death and human sacrifice. Further, it was the desire to escape the death cults of the Aztecs and Mayas, she implies, that drove the ancestors of the modern Pueblo Indians north from their original home in Mexico, before the prophesied arrival of the equally bloodthirsty Europeans.

Perhaps more than any other Western writer, Silko reveals the dialogic connections between European and Indian myths as they have developed in the New World. Indian stories lurk here in the liminal spaces of Anglo America's most beloved narratives, with nearly as much power as the Anglo myths wield in the lives of Indians. Along with the Geronimo stories, for instance, Silko includes a related series about famous American outlaws, especially those who have been mythologized and romanticized by the American public. Sterling, who "had been interested in the law since he was a kid in Indian boarding school. Because everything the white teachers had said and done to the Indian children had been 'required by law,'" (26) has spent a lifetime studying American law and its application. The *Police Gazette* and *True Detective* give him the most detailed explanations of the law, and through decades of reading both magazines, he has realized that most of the outlaw heroes mythologized as Robin Hoods by Anglos were actually Indians. Pretty Boy Floyd, who "struck back at bankers who were taking small farms and leaving Floyd's people homeless during the . . . Great Depression" (27) and who was actually protected from the F.B.I. by local sheriffs, was part Oklahoma Indian. "Floyd's stronghold had been in the brushy oak hill country of Indian Territory. Ma Barker had been part Creek Indian, and John Dillinger's girlfriend, Billy Frechette, had been a Canadian Indian" (27).

Thanks to his magazines, Sterling is aware that many of these famous Indian outlaws had legitimate grievances with the U.S. government, but he is not surprised that while most white Americans would instantly recognize the names of these outlaw heroes, very few would realize they were Indians. Sterling understands this, however, because he knows that those who write histories and guide the generation of myths "preferred that Indians got left out of that part of American history too, since their only other appearances had been at so-called massacres of white settlers" (40).

Most Anglos don't realize that their own myths are intertwined, even dependent, on Indians, but while the Indians are more aware of the hybridized and impure natures of their own cultures, they seem equally unable to step outside the powerful walls of myth continually making and re-making their worlds. Instead, as with many subaltern groups, they attempt to assert their identity by alternately destroying and appropriating for themselves the signs of authority and imperial power they both covet and despise. Those signs are reified and transmitted through the mythic narratives by which each side tries to understand their history and justify their actions. But the threads of those mythic stories have become so tangled and closely interwoven, any attempt to separate or purify one strand inevitably alters and even destroys others. The effect of this is to create image upon image of a world of myths and stories mixed and hybridized, despite the longing of each group for an impossible-to-achieve purity, for the unattainable erasure of the Other who both haunts and structures their world.

St. Clair argues that the almanac, as a collection of connected ancient stories and sacred myths, and the novel *Almanac*, which she calls "an apparent miscellany of isolated stories that gradually assumes design in the reader's consciousness," create a "growing awareness of interconnection" (152) between all human beings. I would argue, however, that consciously or not, Silko has constructed a text that negates that possibility by its very desire for it or, more specifically, by the dual expressions of that desire in the form of the traditional Western, which seeks the disappearance of the Indian followed by the establishment of an untainted (white) civilization, and the Indian almanac, which seeks the disappearance of Anglos followed by the establishment of an untainted (Indian) civilization.

The almanac's central myth, its most important and often-repeated prophecy, is the ironic inverse of the Anglo myth of vanishing Indians, promising that "all traces of Europeans in America would disappear" (632). And yet, as St. Clair notes and as every element in the novel comes together to demonstrate, neither group can ever be eliminated. The attempt to do so is merely the continuation of the savage war that has bound the groups inextricably together in the first place. The "growing awareness of interconnection" appears not to draw people together in peace but conversely to drive them to more and more desperate and violent enactments of "cowboys and indians," continuing bloody expressions of a savage war that blindly seeks to destroy the very thing upon which it depends for its existence. What Said describes as a puzzling paradox—an American discourse "more policed, more anxious to depict the country as free from taint, more unified around one ironclad major narrative of innocent triumph" (314–15)—is not really puzzling at all. It is the futile but insistent denial of the realization that there has never been, and can never be, an "innocent triumph" in a savage war.

Even Silko seems to realize this truth. In his hopeless perusal of pop psychology magazines, Sterling reads that doctors advise depressed people to put their pasts behind them, to forget what is dead and gone and focus only on the present, as though the past truly is dead and has no effect on the present. La Escapia, listening to the lectures of the Communist Cuban, realizes this is exactly what whites have been telling Indians to do for centuries. But her tribe's elders insist that the past cannot be forgotten or ignored; "they must reckon with the past because within it lay seeds of the present and future. They must reckon with the past because within it lay this present moment and also the future moment" (311).

This realization is perhaps one aspect of what drives modern America's fascination with the mythic narratives underlying Westerns, as well as our stubborn attempts to repeat, revise, and rewrite those myths. It is certainly the motivating factor in the assemblage and preservation of the almanac. Yet even as La Escapia reflects that "No matter what you or anyone else did . . . history would catch up with you; it was inevitable, it was relentless" (316), she is organizing the collection and distribution of assault rifles, rocket launchers, and stolen military helicopters to turn against Europeans in yet another cycle in the savage war, seeking what she feels to be a justified exercise of physical violence. She seems incapable of seeing that she is an actor in a myth, participating in the continuing creation of yet another version of "the narrative of innocent triumph."

In the end, if this novel creates any sense of interdependence, it is less between peoples than their various myths, between their shared pasts and their intimately connected present, between history and the future. And yet unlike Tayo's deliberate step away from violence in the final scenes of *Ceremony* through his decision not to kill Emo despite what most Americans would consider ample justification, *Almanac* offers no such nonviolent possibility. The savage war, now locked into the interdependent, or perhaps co-dependent, structures of both Anglo and Indian myths, seems to have become the dominant force directing the various cultures battling each other for possession of the future and the past of the Americas. While Said posits such violent eruptions of nationalistic separatist movements demonstrate a fundamental liberationist energy, Silko seems to suggest that such a decolonizing move is impossible, negated by the very imperialist process of mythic hybridization that created it.

CHAPTER 6

Necessary Difference

The Creation of a Chicana Utopia in Ana Castillo's *So Far from God*

> *The difference between the colonial and decolonial imaginaries is that the colonial retains the inhibiting trace, accepting power relations as they are . . . not reconfiguring them. . . . The decolonial imaginary challenges power relations to decolonize notions of otherness to move into a liberatory terrain.*
>
> EMMA PÉREZ

Like many other Western novels, *So Far from God* is essentially concerned with space—geographic, metaphysical, cultural, and spiritual. Previous chapters in this work have examined the myth of the frontier as it was traditionally utilized in the claiming of territory through justified violence in the quest to establish an imperial space. *So Far from God* imagines how the myth of the frontier may be used by the subaltern subject as well as the dominant culture(s) to shape the space thus claimed. The quest for a new Eden through the founding of a white utopia in the wilderness of the New World is, of course, the major justification of the frontier experience and at the heart of the imperial project. Mythologized as both the reason and reward for fighting the savage war, the utopia in the golden West is a longstanding icon in literature from and about the region. This is especially true in writings by Anglo women, as Annette Kolodny has noted. The claiming and shaping of wilderness as garden has been a common trope in figuring the space of the West (both mythic and geographic) as utopic and female. This construction has generally supported the typical mythic vision of the West as being transformed from savage wilderness to utopic garden only upon settlement by Europeans. It does provide at the same time, however, a counter construction to the typical mythic vision of the West as a male-dominated space shaped exclusively by war and violence.

The quest for a utopic space takes somewhat different forms in white and Hispanic versions, although they are closely related. Each version must somehow glorify the savage war needed to wrest that space from its original inhabitants and at the same time mask the morally troubling reality of invasion and theft underlying that war. The birth of the modern Chicano Movement, which brought with it a consciousness for Chicanos of being both colonizers and colonized, resulted in changes to their mythic stories of the utopic West, at once subverting and upholding the rationales of imperialism such myths provide. While the actual geographic location of the utopia born of the savage war shifts under the hands of different authors and different times, since el Movimiento, for Ana Castillo and many Chicanos, it is located in the Mexican American borderlands.[1] Gloria Anzaldúa defines this region as a sort of third country. For its Chicano inhabitants, she says, it is the source of "a shock culture, a border culture" (11) that is part of the dominant cultures of the United States and Mexico and yet wholly accepted by neither.

The borderlands of *So Far from God* form a shifting and slippery space that, like the border in Silko's *Almanac,* both divides and unites those who traverse it and that significantly marks them, as well. These borderlands are not simply a line between countries or cultures that can be easily or completely crossed; rather they are, as Anzaldúa calls them, a third country, a colonized and often dangerous space, a site of cultural, racial, and linguistic contention and violence. And yet paradoxically, Castillo suggests, also the only space in which Chicanas can hope to find their new Eden. This cannot occur, however, until some new mythic structure alters the power relationships inherent in the colonial imaginary defining the space of the Borderlands and begins, as Pérez puts it, "to decolonize notions of otherness to move into a liberatory terrain" (110).

Theorists like Anzaldúa, Chela Sándoval, Maria Herrera-Sobek, and Ramón Saldívar have long identified America's borderlands as sites of liminality, sources of forbidden pleasure, both dangerous and desirable. Victor Turner, Mary Douglas, and others remind us that borders, be they social, geographic, or psychological, exist to define the self, in part by defining what is *not* the self, what is beyond and across, alien and other. And yet as they also note, the prize to be won from venturing to such sites and braving the pollution of contact with them is power. The continued production of myths from and about America's border regions is an acknowledgement that those issues that constructed historic frontiers have not disappeared into the mythologized past. Just as in the past, those individuals who venture into or inhabit the forbidden, for whatever reasons, are marked with both pollution and power, seen by the dominant culture(s) as somehow impure but paradoxically necessary for the founding and defense of the utopic space sought on the other side of that frontier.[2] Frontiers are more than simply sites of first contact and borderlands more than third countries separating and joining disparate cultures; they are dangerous, powerful places, attractive and repellant in their determined insistence on the existence of an Other, a space outside or beyond, often seen as threatening to negate the longed-for utopia and the safely contained identities thought to be found within it.

The American fascination with its frontiers and borderlands becomes a fascination with its own Otherness, an acknowledgment of the powerful zones within and against which identities are defined, cultures and communities created and perpetuated. Thus the Southwest as metaphorical home of American's borderlands, both savage frontier and mythic utopia, is often seen as the locus of the most passionately contentious battles over those issues that decide the shape of our identities and the borders that surround them. Such dangerous and contentious sites, however, are more easily dealt with at a safe remove. As Patricia Limerick notes, the Southwest has traditionally been viewed as a distant frontier far removed geographically from the center of "real" American life. At the same time, she argues, the region is seen as the holder of "a potent and persistent variety of nationalistic myth" (30), a special, Edenic, mythic place in which "the public holds to the idea of a great discontinuity between the [historic] frontier and the Western present" (31). This discontinuity, an imaginary separation or distinction between past and present, acts as a sort of safety buffer, allowing the frontier of the past, the mythical or historically imagined Southwest, to function as a stage upon which the problems and issues wracking the modern borderlands and the rest of the nation can be restaged, reenacted, and refigured at a safe remove. Thus battles over issues such as land use and the environment, immigration, and bilingualism and English-only legislation, what Limerick terms "the legacy of conquest," seem to be concentrated in the Southwest in a curious act of acknowledgement of that legacy and denial of its historic and current relevance. The bones of the power structures the process of decolonization seeks to dismantle are particularly close to the surface here, only barely hidden by the protective buffer of historical discontinuity.

That buffer, like all borders, is disturbingly permeable. The function of borders, especially in Chicano literature, has often been ambivalent and contradictory. As Annamarie Jagose remarks in her reading of Anzaldúa's *Borderlands/La Frontera: The New Mestiza,* figures of racial and cultural hybridity produced in the borderlands are often represented as somehow transcending difference, escaping from the borderlands and their conflicting function of "slash and suture" (213). In reality, Jagose argues, "that hybrid [the mestiza] . . . who is at once similar and different, does not move beyond, but replicates the function of, the border" (224). In Anzalúa's attempt to install the mestiza beyond distinction and demarcation, as a hybrid mother of a new race that will eliminate difference, Jagose argues, she ignores the border's "internal resistance to utopic recuperation" (212). In other words, despite Anzaldúa's attempt to establish the mestiza as a new Eve in a borderlands Eden, Jagose claims she is ultimately thwarted by the very nature of the borderlands themselves, as a space that, contrary to most utopic visions, serves to highlight difference and distinction, to reify the instability of identity and the impossibility of cultural or racial purity. And, as Joan Penzenstadler says, with the exception of the works of Rudolfo Anaya (and, I will argue, Ana Castillo) most Chicano literature is anti-utopic, unable to reconcile the desire for a more stable and less threatened identity with the inherently unstable nature of the borderlands and the contradictory freedom such a kinetic space offers.

Genaro Padilla speculates that one reason for this may be that "the historical situation has for over a century produced a rhetorical site upon which Chicano literary production has had as one of its generative principles the reconciling of vexing contradictions. . . . we see again and again a narrative ground (often a battleground) upon which an individual is contending with social, cultural, and ideological forces that simultaneously so disrupt identity as to unfix it yet, paradoxically, in disrupting identity establish identity as a destabilized condition" (11). In fact, as Sarah McWilliams asserts, although borderlands can become imprisoned in the "oppressive economy of duality ('us' vs. 'them') . . . they can also be seen as the space from which differences emerge as positive forces for change. As a catalytic space for the renegotiation and fracturing of absolute categories, the multicultural constitution of the borderlands keeps differences intact" (74).

So the borderlands, those outside boundaries that give shape to the imagined utopia beyond them, while both colonized and dangerous, also allow for (or perhaps demand) a redefinition and revision of culture, self, and identity where inhabitants can be concomitantly one *and* the Other. Unable, in a decolonizing space, to entirely escape the effects of conquest and imperialism, indeed often both agent and victim of it, the inhabitants of the borderlands must create a mythic vision in direct contradiction to the traditional idea of a utopia in which cultural and social purity are presumed to result in a wholeness of self and identity. Rather, as Castillo has done in *So Far from God,* utopia itself is reimagined as a hybridized, differentiated space producing identities that are fractured, shifting, and unfixed.

Traditionally, identity is perceived to spring from undivided utopic spaces often far removed in time or space from the reality of the imperial present in the United States. Thus we see a constant and often violently passionate debate over identifiers: Mexican or Mexican American? Chicano or Hispanic? Latina or Spanish or Spanish American? These are the labels that attempt to locate identity, to fix it and make it (more or less) stable. The desire for stability often grounds identity in a romanticized, mythologized Old World space perceived as being outside the modern borderlands, a space often assumed to be somehow more culturally homogenous or pure. In most utopic visions, whether of a romanticized Old World or a brave new one, homogeneity rather than hybridity or difference is the goal.[3]

In the borderlands, however, as McWilliams implies, difference can become something else. The erasure or transcendence of difference would require the borderlands identity to simply merge with the dominant cultural identity on one or the other side of the border, or in the case of Anzaldúa's mestiza, demand that both sides merge seamlessly into an undifferentiated middle. For those caught between the two sides, however, difference can become a necessary tool for cultural- and self-definition, wielded by the borderlands inhabitants to craft a new, postmodern vision of identity, one that balances, however paradoxically, the "vexing contradictions" Padilla identifies as inherent in Chicano literature and experience. This is the first step in the process of mythogenesis necessary for beginning the decolonization of the borderlands space and the colonized/colonizing borderlands subject.

This requires a radical revision of traditional notions of utopia, which Castillo has undertaken in *So Far from God.* To create a utopic borderlands, both functions of the border—slash and suture, undifferentiation and distinction—must be preserved, not erased or transcended. Castillo attempts this contradictory venture by constructing her borderlands as a site that does not translate from one dominant culture to another nor disappear in a new and undifferentiated global hybrid; rather her borderlands enable a relationship between both sides of the border without erasing the distinction of the space within, a sort of neutral territory where difference is both produced and preserved. Chela Sándoval names this "differential consciousness . . . a kinetic motion that maneuvers, poetically transfigures, and orchestrates while demanding alienation, perversion and reformation. . . . it permits functioning within yet beyond the demands of dominant ideology" (3).

The situating of utopic sites in the Southwest has a contentious history in Chicano culture and studies. Aztec myths located Aztlán (the utopic homeland from which the Aztecs traveled south to found their capital, Tenochtitlan, near present-day Mexico City), somewhere far to the north. Chicano activists in the 1960s and 1970s seized on this myth, situating the edenic Aztlán in what is now the border region of the American Southwest, developing it as a symbol that could unite Chicanos while legitimizing Chicano presence in the United States in the face of Anglo hostility. Some claim that Aztlán, which roughly translates as "place of the herons," refers to the vast wetlands now called Bosque del Apache south of Albuquerque, New Mexico, which is a major resting place on the migratory path of North American herons.

While certainly well aware of this mythic Chicano Eden in the Southwest, Castillo avoids mentioning Aztlán directly in *So Far from God,* despite setting much of the action of the novel in and around Albuquerque, in the mythical town of Tome. Possible reasons for this reticence are many. Daniel Cooper Alarcón notes in *The Aztec Palimpsest* that "As a political symbol of Chicano cultural nationalism, Aztlán has been linked to and used to legitimize Chicano identity. However, critics of el Movimiento have criticized the ideology symbolized by Aztlán as monolithic and unresponsive to many of the members it sought to encompass" (7). The protective and encompassing umbrella of Aztlán, Cooper Alarcón argues, has obscured a number of issues important to Chicano identity, particularly those surrounding gender, class, and sexuality, the very issues Castillo engages in *So Far from God.* In fact, *So Far,* like much of Castillo's earlier novel, *Sapogonia,* offers a rather blunt critique of many aspects of Chicano activism and Chicano culture, including the roles of women in each. Pérez argues that by taking the image of Aztlán as its founding myth, el Movimiento dooms itself to a specific Chicano nationalism rooted in patriarchal discourse and activism where "nationalism becomes a return to the mother—Aztlán—where woman can be only metaphor and object" (122).

As in Silko's work, the border region here is seen, at least by its non-Anglo inhabitants, as a center, a heartland rather than a distant frontier. For the dominant cultures of the United States and Mexico, New Mexico may be a frontier region and the far edge of civilization, but for the Nuevo Mexicanos, it is the median, the overlapping and doubled heartland of both north and south, Spanish and English, Mexican and Anglo American cultures. It is crossed, supported, and demarcated by the often conflicting cultures brought together by American, Spanish, and Mexican imperialism in the region. Alvina Quintana notes that Chicano culture, caught between opposing extremes, "has been labeled by anthropologists as a 'creole culture' because it draws on two or more origins" (74). The mythic Chicano utopia imagined by Castillo in *So Far from God* exists in a creole space, a landscape molded and shaped by multiple cultures, multiple visions of the region's history and future, and defined by complexly intertwined versions of the myth of utopia in the golden West. The identities of her characters are defined by their struggle to create a new mythic narrative by which to structure a utopic space that negates neither the Mexican, Anglo, or Chicano cultures fighting to control it but does not surrender to them either. This anti-utopic utopia of impurity and cultural hybridity is called Chicanía by Joan Penzenstadler, "an intermediate zone, . . . perceived in terms of Anglo-Hispanic contrasts at either of its edges. Fronting Mexico, Chicanía and its Mexican American inhabitants have a relatively Anglo character; fronting the rest of the United States—Gringuía—Chicanía is by comparison 'Mexican'" (162). The defining characteristic of the borderlands for the inhabitants of Castillo's novel is their difference, and their major task is to find a way to live with but not destroy that difference.

Quintana identifies this aspect of Borderlands existence as especially important for Chicana authors, who, she says,

> find themselves resisting not one but two oppositional discourses which deny them visibility, [thus] they are confronted with a complex dilemma. If they choose to break their silence, they are faced with the prospect of developing a liberation strategy that either sells out to one of these outside forces or contributes to a new perspective which is influenced by, but not limited to either Anglo-feminist or traditional Chicano ideologies. On the positive side of this equation, this marginal position . . . provides the writers with the strategic position to enhance or refute two outside sources and thereby contribute to the emergence of a new culture, a culture which by its very nature is characterized by a multiplicity of voices and experiences. (258)

The preservation of this multiplicity and difference, and the complexity of the balancing act required to juggle such perpetually shifting, multilayered identities, is demonstrated by Castillo in the title of her novel. It is taken from a quote originally uttered by Mexican President Porfirio Diaz: "Pity poor Mexico, so far from God, so close to the United States." In Chicanía New Mexico, this phrase has been, like the culture of los Nuevo Mexicanos, creolized, hybridized, and altered to fit the reality of the modern borderlands and is commonly quoted as "Pity poor New Mexico, so far from God, so close to Texas." This serves as a synecdoche of Chicano culture, a dialectical mirroring of the historical original that, in its altered form, both reflects and refers to its birth in Mexico and simultaneously speaks to the reality of life north of the border. The new phrase, often uttered in the new language, in effect doubles the meaning of the old, acknowledging not only anti-Mexican sentiment in the United States, especially during the Mexican revolution when Diaz is said to have made the original quote, but at the same time pointing to the anti-Mexican sentiment still associated with Texas and to Texas' history of persecution of its Mexican, and later Mexican American, population.

The phrase locates the speaker and the speaker's culture in a difficult-to-define space, at once far from God (implying some metaphysical place of spiritual safety from which the speaker is removed) and close to something else (a dangerous and hostile region). Physical geography and spiritual geography are collapsed and conflated here, with the speaker inhabiting some space betwixt and between, neither wholly here nor there, and yet existing in both spaces at once, linguistically, racially, and culturally both Mexican and American, but not entirely one or the other. Castillo intends, I believe, yet other layers of meaning, implying at least a partial separation from the monolithic structure of the Catholic church and a rejection of the Church's vision of a patriarchal utopia, as well as a separation from the monolithic structures of Mexican, Chicano, and Anglo American cultures and a rejection of their visions of a homogenized, unified cultural utopia.

The borderlands then, for Castillo's Chicano characters, are both a heartland where the multiple influences of Mexico and the United States converge and combine and an interstices, a contested and colonized center caught between two nations within which inhabitants struggle to define their identities, sometimes with and sometimes against the dominant cultures. As Quintana notes, the resulting Chicano culture bears the marks of north and south as well as the scars of battling each. For Castillo's female characters there is the additional struggle against the crippling patriarchal colonizations of women in Anglo, Mexican, and Chicano worlds.

Sándoval theorized in "Feminism and Racism" that the oppositional consciousness that subaltern groups must develop in a colonized space produces a particularly "self-conscious flexibility of identity" (66). This results, in

Castillo's novel, in semi-mythic individuals who become saints, spirits, martyrs, or, as Castillo calls them, "chicana international astral-travelers" (162), capable of traversing all boundaries freely, even those of life and death. Indeed, in a dark irony reminiscent of McCarthy's work, it is only through their deaths that Castillo's borderlands utopia is forged.

So Far from God, though set in the American Southwest, is clearly influenced stylistically by the magical realism of Latin American writers. As Castillo notes, early in her career she read many Latin American texts and says she was particularly taken by the works of Gabriel García Márquez and Jorge Amado, as well as Toni Morrison, whose novels also contain elements of magical realism.[4] According to Castillo, her novel was inspired by a story from medieval Christian mythology, an allegorical tale involving Sophia (wisdom) and her three daughters, Faith, Hope, and Charity.[5] At the end of the original myth, Sophia/Wisdom stands weeping over the graves of her three allegorical daughters, hopelessly resigned to the stubborn, unchanging sinfulness of human nature. In *So Far from God,* Castillo revisions this myth, creolizes it like the revised Mexican dicho of her title, mixing it with traditional Mexican and Indian myths and recrafting it into an allegory of the borderlands, a lesson for learning from and living with the differences constructing the modern borderlands space. The result, like the borderlands itself, is both tragic and utopic, earthly and spiritual, a complex and contradictory mythic vision.

The revisioning of myths is a hallmark of much literature produced by colonized peoples. Trinh Min-ha writes that "To listen carefully is to preserve. But to preserve is to burn, for understanding means creating" (121). For colonized peoples, especially the often doubly colonized woman of color, survival means not necessarily preserving old stories, myths, and traditional visions of what a utopia should be and how it should look (although it may mean knowing them); rather it demands retelling, creating new myths and new visions from the ashes of the old. The retelling of myths is a powerful means of reconstituting history, the world born from it, and the identities of those who inhabit colonized, conquered, borderland spaces. These reconstituted myths often appear in versions that reverse or destroy the unitary identities most commonly found in European and Anglo American literature and that are sought by most utopic visions. Donna Haraway calls those who recraft such myths "cyborg authors" (175), ones who inhabit a forbidden and hybridized zone and are themselves mixed and impure, sign and symbol of crossed borders. Haraway argues that "In re-telling . . . stories, cyborg authors subvert the central myths of origin of Western culture. We have all been colonized by those origin myths" (175). In typical narratives these mixed and impure cyborgs would be anti-utopic characters that must somehow be assimilated or destroyed, their differences erased, to create or preserve utopia.

Stuart Hall, in his discussion of the representation and cultural identity of Caribbean peoples, calls the identity produced by and from the post-colonial space a "diaspora identity . . . defined, not by essence or purity, but by the recognition of a necessary heterogeneity, diversity . . . by *hybridity* [emphasis in original]. Diaspora identities are those which are constantly producing and reproducing themselves anew, through transformation and difference" (80). Castillo attempts to build her utopic vision from this kinetic and unstable space, albeit a decolonizing rather than post-colonial one. She is not always successful. The continued diaspora from Mexico into the United States, for example, is virtually ignored here. Only one character in the novel is directly associated with Mexico, and she is a legal immigrant who has been in the United States for decades. As Cooper Alarcón has noted, this is another issue running like a faultline through Chicano communities obscured by the utopic vision of Aztlán and equally obscured and ignored by Castillo. Her single Mexican character is an idealized, Chicanoized vision of Mexico, a traditional curandera who has nonetheless traveled extensively in Europe and speaks Spanish, French, and English. This character manages to embody all the romance of Old Mexico safely and legally ensconced in the United States, untainted by any of the messier issues like illegal immigration and green cards attached to many recent and less well-educated arrivals.

The curandera, Doña Felicia, does, however, serve as a fascinating example of the hybridity of identity mentioned by Hall by acting as a sort of living meeting place between the supposedly irreconcilable worlds of European Roman Catholicism and indigenous native religions. As many have noted, the folk Catholicism commonly practiced in much of the U.S. Southwest and Mexico is not the original Roman Catholicism of Europe but a borderlands version, mixed with Native American images and beliefs. The bultos crafted by New Mexican santeros or painted on church walls, for instance, often appear with native images of holiness, such as ears of corn, eagles, and stylized suns. Doña Felicia, who heals with herbs and spells and offers protection against curses and the evil eye, also attends mass regularly and holds highly honored duties in the church, though this sort of hybridization is not entirely to the liking of Rome.

The death and resurrection of the youngest daughter of Castillo's modern-day Sofia, who is known thereafter as La Loca, illustrates the dangers of inhabiting a borderlands space not yet decolonized. When parishioners at

Doña Felicia's church witness the little girl's miraculous resurrection at her own funeral mass, she is instantly named a saint, despite the protests of the Anglo priest. However, as McCarthy demonstrated in *The Crossing,* once one has crossed the borders, one is forever marked with difference, unable to return to a state of purity. La Loca is already marked in Anglo culture as a brown-skinned Chicana, a borderlands inhabitant racially, culturally, and linguistically. But having transgressed the boundaries of life and death, she is marked yet again. She learns to recognize the smell of death during her time as a corpse and now cannot bear to be near any other human beings, all of whom reek of the grave to her. She flees when anyone other than her mother approaches her. She is raised in complete isolation on her mother's small farm outside of Tome, never attending school or interacting with other people, but spending her time talking to the farm animals, to her imaginary playmate (who turns out to be the mythical spirit/ghost known as La Llorona), praying, and having prophetic dreams. Her prayers are truly powerful and help to heal her sisters Caridad (Charity) and Fe (Faith), and her dreams are always accurate, but her power is paid for by social ostracism.

As a teenager, Loca dies from AIDS, though she is a virgin and has had no physical contact with another human being, not even her mother, since her resurrection. Her infection is a mystery, and this serves to cast her as a martyr, forcing her community to confront the AIDS epidemic free from divisive and distracting issues of blame or guilt directed at victims perceived as being sexually deviant, promiscuous, or users of illegal drugs. After her death, La Loca communicates with her mother and appears to the faithful around the world. A shrine is built to her, and her image is plastered on holy candles, showing La Loca dressed in flowing blue robes like the Virgen de Guadalupe, although the robe is actually a blue chenille bathrobe she wore for her participation in the procession of the Stations of the Cross on Holy Friday. She becomes known in masses as "Patrona de los Hambrientes, Patrona de las Enfermedades Misteriosas" [Patroness of the Starving, Patroness of Mysterious Diseases] (249), and "it was considered a good idea to have a little statue of La Loca in your kitchen and to give one as a good luck gift to new brides and progressive grooms" (248).

La Loca Santa, the virgin saint from the South Valley, becomes a sort of modern Chicana Virgen de Guadalupe, down to the typical blue robes in which the brown-skinned Virgin is generally depicted. Like the Virgen de Guadalupe, she is a mixed and hybridized saint, reflecting her borderlands identity. She wears her blue bathrobe, sign of her sainthood, over battered Levis, a man's plaid Pendelton shirt, and a pair of cowboy boots. She speaks in a combination of English and Spanish and makes her famous procession, as befits a Western saint, on horseback. Though never recognized by Rome, she is nonetheless a powerful symbol for other borderlands inhabitants, squeezing through the cracks of the dominant culture's religion and acting from the space between.

La Loca is not one of the three daughters in the original myth that inspired Castillo's novel. She is perhaps best seen as the spontaneous expression of the spiritual beliefs—part Roman Catholicism, part folk religion, and a blend of Mexican, Native American, and Anglo—of the Chicano community as a whole. This is a utopia influenced by, but ultimately independent from, the Church in Rome. Like those who believe in her, this utopia's saint bears the marks of her borderlands origins. The paradox of her life and death, a virgin who has lived the life of a holy hermit yet who dies of AIDS, mirrors the conundrum of life in the borderlands. La Loca is both pure and polluted, monstrous in her crazy antisocial behavior, yet a martyr and saint who prays for her people in life and becomes their holy intermediary in death. Like the slippery space of the borderlands, she confounds easy categorization, rejecting a unitary identity for a contradictory Otherness.

Esperanza (Hope), on the other hand, finds herself constantly at odds with the Church, Chicano culture, and Anglo culture. Rather than living in physical isolation and spiritual openness like La Loca, Esperanza is physically immersed in the world, sexually and politically, but spiritually lost and confused. Castillo writes, "In high school, although a rebel, she was Catholic heart and soul. In college, she had a romance with marxism, but was still Catholic. In graduate school, she was atheist and, in general, a cynic. Lately, she prayed to Grandmother Earth and Grandfather Sky. For good measure, however, she had been reading a flurry of self-help books" (38). Esperanza moves from battle to battle, fighting to cross the social, cultural, and gender borders that structure her world. It would appear she has achieved the American dream—money, success, and fame—Anglo America's version of utopia. Yet the borders she violates to reach these goals mark her as much as they do her sister, La Loca.

Esperanza searches for a means to reconcile the competing differences in her life through romance but fails. Most Anglo men, she finds, are put off by her political activism as a Chicana, as are those traditional Hispanic men who reject the politically controversial label "Chicano" for the more neutral "Spanish" or "Hispanic," while men of both cultures are intimidated by her political activism as a feminist. She ends up dating a Chicano named Ruben "who during the height of his Chicano cosmic consciousness, renamed himself

Cuauhtemoc" (25). She lives with him while she is in college, "despite her mother's opposition, who said of her eldest daughter's nonsanctified union: 'Why should a man buy the cow when he can have the milk for free?' 'I am not a cow,' Esperanza responded, but despite this, right after graduation Cuauhtemoc dumped her for a middle-class gabacha [white girl] with a Corvette; they bought a house in the Northeast Heights in Albuquerque right after their wedding" (25–26). Esperanza leaves the relatively safe and contained world of Tome and her mother's house for the powerful, alien world of Anglo culture. By leaving the borderlands space where difference, even before the revisioning of that space as a new sort of utopia, is recognized and more or less accommodated, she becomes an outsider, a trespasser culturally and, through her Chicano activism, politically. However, as her life demonstrates, even within Chicanía, some differences are more acceptable than others. When Ruben's marriage to the gabacha falls apart, Esperanza resumes her relationship with him.

> Every two weeks she was right there with Ruben, at the teepee meeting of the Native-American Church, Ruben singing and drumming, keeping the fire, watching the "door," teaching her the do's and don't's of his interpretation of lodge "etiquette" and the role of women and the role of men and how they were not to be questioned. . . . After all, there was Ruben with his Native and Chicano male friends always joking among themselves, always siding with each other, and always agreeing about the order and reason of the universe, and since Esperanza had no Native women friends to verify any of what was being told to her by Ruben about the woman's role in what they were doing, she did not venture to contradict him. . . . Afterward they went home and made love all day. The problem was that then she would not hear from Ruben again until the next time there was a meeting. She was beginning to feel like part of a ritual in which she herself participated as an unsuspecting symbol, like a staff or a rattle or medicine. (36)

And she is right, of course. Esperanza's life up to this point is a sort of allegory of the boundaries confining and defining the world of Chicanas. Like Esperanza, they may hope that education, careers, or financial success will free them from the suffocating gender roles imposed by Mexican, Chicano, and Anglo cultures or allow them to transcend the racial and linguistic prejudices of the Anglo world, but those borders that reject rather than accept difference follow them wherever they go. Indeed, like Esperanza, they may simply be trading one set of boundaries for another, equally rigid. If education is held out to the woman of color in America as her hope for transcending borders, Castillo's version of Hope implies it is an empty promise and that Chicanas cannot hope to attain utopia through someone else's myth.

But the promise may be equally unrealizable for men. Ruben here is both colonized and colonizer, reclaiming his indigenous heritage though never able to acknowledge that the mixed blood that flows through his veins is the result of a conquest by Spain as brutal and bloodthirsty as that of the "gabachos" he both despises and desires. He chooses the Aztec name Cuauhtemoc to help him define his new identity as a politically active Chicano in an obvious reference to the legacy of Aztlán. Castillo makes clear, however, that it is a hollow gesture, political but not personal in nature, and therefore a thin and easily penetrated facade but one that nonetheless gives Ruben tacit permission to mistreat Esperanza, protected by his mask of political correctness and "Chicano cosmic consciousness."

It also serves to mask the complex history of Ruben's ancestry by focusing on his Indian racial heritage (Castillo implies he has no real concept of a true cultural heritage here) while conspicuously erasing the rest of his forebears. This is, according to Penzenstadler, common in Chicano fiction, which, "following its own mythical view of things, chooses virtually to ignore the Spaniards as progenitors and to concentrate on the Native American side of the ancestry" (159–60). Castillo subverts this aspect of Chicano literature and el Movimiento through Ruben's fashionable fascination with his indigenous heritage. His pilgrimages to Mayan sites in Mexico and his participation in the sweats are presented as a kind of cheap, spiritual tourism, a method of appropriating what he wants from native cultures without having to attempt to understand them in any meaningful or significant way and that allows him to ignore the reality of the Spanish conquest. He, and by implication el Movimiento, turns this expropriation into a weapon to wield against Esperanza, to colonize her as woman, as Chicana, as India, to in fact ritualize her colonization by making her into a ritual object to be controlled, to force her to participate in the ceremony of her own domination. Anglo, Mexican, Native American, and Chicano cultures all conspire here under the questionable utopic symbol of Aztlán to dominate the woman caught between them.

Ruben does ironic double duty here in pointing to hypocrisies in several places. His romantic and nostalgic invocation of a mythologized past is virtually identical to that often found in autobiographies of Mexican Americans from the late nineteenth and early twentieth centuries. Such writers, Genaro Padilla notes, almost exclusively from a wealthy and landed gentry, produced a body of work in which "nostalgia for an earlier cultural configuration is the central feature" (x). "But the more I read," he continues, "the more I came to realize that by the end of the nineteenth century just about the only estate left to any of our antepasados was one situated in the geography of the past" (x). While Ruben and the politically minded Chicanos with whom he associates would doubtless have nothing but contempt for ricos who would romanticize an hacienda-laden past in which poor farmers were exploited and abused, he nonetheless finds himself (and by implication, Castillo suggests, the Chicano movement) in an identical position, inextricably bound to a past embodied by the utopic, albeit constricting, myth of Aztlán, unable to accommodate the conflicting realities of Spanish and Indian blood, of antepasados who were both colonizers and colonized, exploiters and exploited, and of a modern reality even more mixed and hybridized, shot through with class, gender, racial, and cultural difference. Instead, he discovers, as with Padilla's autobiographers, that the only estate left to him is one "situated in the geography of the past," which has been carefully edited to present a mythic vision that seeks the very cultural purity and undifferentiated identity Castillo suggests is inimical to utopia in a decolonizing borderlands space.

This vision of Chicano history and culture, Cooper Alarcón argues, "has failed to take into account the diversity of the Chicano experience . . . and instead has emphasized a collective Chicano experience that minimizes class, gender, and regional differences while romanticizing the past" (6). As a result, he claims, Chicanos today stand at a crossroads that seem to offer only two possible paths: one continuing the "tendency to romanticize the past; the other choice, usually resulting from a negative reaction to such nostalgia, rejects the past, particularly the mythic past, as irrelevant to the concerns of the present. Both approaches are flawed" (6).

Castillo attempts, through the story of each of Sofia's daughters, to establish her Chicana utopia between these two spaces, with the fate of each daughter illustrating the dangers to be found in straying onto one or the other road. Unable to find a suitable identity within the mythologized past offered her by Ruben, Esperanza attempts escape by grasping the utopic promise of Anglo culture, the American dream of success, rejecting the mythic past as irrelevant. She leaves Ruben, accepts a job with a TV news station in Washington, D.C., and goes to Kuwait to cover the Gulf War. But she is again betrayed by an empty promise. She is captured, tortured, and murdered in the Middle East after being held for months as a prisoner of war, ignored by an American government unconcerned with the fate of a brown-skinned woman.

Esperanza does not disappear from the world completely, however. She sends La Llorona to communicate the news of her death to her sister, La Loca. "Who better but La Llorona could the spirit of Esperanza have found," Castillo writes, "if not a woman who had been given a bad rap by every generation of her people since the beginning of time and yet, to Esperanza's spirit-mind, La Llorona in the beginning (before men got in the way of it all) may have been nothing short of a loving mother goddess" (162–63). The figure of La Llorona, the weeping woman crying on the banks of rivers and arroyos for the children she murdered, said to call to lone travelers and disobedient youngsters in order to lure them to their death, is a complicated figure in Chicano literature, and her redemption and revisioning at Castillo's hands is a fascinating synecdoche for Castillo's redemption and revisioning of utopia. La Llorona is, according to most versions of this myth, an adulteress as well as a murderess, a woman who drowns her children rather than allowing them to be taken from her by her husband, and her ghost is doomed to eternal wandering because of her crimes. Stories of La Llorona, originally of Mexican origin and long a part of Chicano culture, have now begun appearing in Native American folktales on both sides of the border.

Castillo, like other Chicana writers, connects La Llorona with La Malinche. For Chicana writers, the story of La Malinche is an especially potent origin myth. The historic Malinche is believed to have been a member of a tribe conquered by the Aztecs, sold to them as a slave around the age of fourteen by her parents, then given by the Aztecs to Cortez as a concubine. She spoke several Indian languages, quickly learned Spanish, and acted as his interpreter. According to the myth, she betrayed the secrets of the Aztec's great city and their emperor to Cortez and the Spaniards, earning her the title of La Chingada, literally "the fucked one." Anzaldúa writes, "She has become the bad word that passes a dozen times a day from the lips of Chicanos. Whore, prostitute, the woman who sold out her people to the Spaniards are epithets Chicanos spit out with contempt" (22). Anzaldúa, however, demands an accounting from the Aztecs who she says betrayed Malinche as a woman, the Spaniards who betrayed her as a dark-skinned Indian, and the Anglos who betray her for being both female and nonwhite. She also demands accounting from Chicanos whose culture she says can "cripple its women, como burras, our strengths used against us, lowly burras bearing humility with dignity. . . . No, I do not buy all the myths of the tribe into which I was born" (21–22). Ruben's behavior as both colonized subject and oppressive colonizer of Esperanza illustrates the contradiction inherent in el Movimiento's appropriation of the myth of Aztlán with its glorification of Indianess and concomitant rejection of it by its repudiation of Malinche, the original Indian mother. Pérez explains that by viewing Malinche as the dreaded phallic mother who will devour, castrate, and usurp the Chicano of his power, "He must therefore ally with the white colonizer father. . . . This dynamic . . . will be the driving force behind a form of patriarchal Chicano nationalism that repudiates feminism" (107). Thus Malinche and her daughters will be despised and colonized over and over, by Anglo, Mexican, and Chicano cultures.

In order to escape this oppressive cycle, the figure of Malinche must be decolonized. In Castillo's retelling, La Malinche is also La Llorona, mourning her lost children, murdered not by her own hand but by the conquerors and colonizers of all races. She is also, as Castillo and others have suggested, the symbolic mother of Chicanos and Mexicanos, giving birth to Cortez's son, who many say was the first offspring between Spaniard and Indian, the original mestizo hybrid. She becomes, therefore, a sort of living human version of the ancient mother goddesses worshipped in both Europe and the Americas. Through her connection to Esperanza (Hope), Malinche/Llorona begins the process of decolonization necessary for recrafting the borderlands into a feminine utopic space. Receiving Esperanza's lectures on political issues and current events from beyond the grave via this mythical figure, Sofia is inspired to run for mayor of Tome and begin the revision of the borderlands that will result in her Chicana utopia.

If Esperanza represents the futile struggles of women and Chicanas in the white and male dominated world of political and economic success, Caridad (Charity) traverses the vicious social borders defining female sexuality. Caridad, as her name suggests, is a giver, and she gives freely of her heart and her body to a stream of men in the cowboy/vaquero bars in Albuquerque's South Valley. All of Anglo, Mexican, and Chicano cultures' anxieties about female sexuality and femininity are embodied in Caridad. She is the sister with "perfect teeth and round, apple-shaped breasts. Unlike the rest of the women in her family who, despite her grandmother's insistence that they were *Spanish* [emphasis in original], descendants of pure Spanish blood, all shared the flat butt of the Pueblo blood undeniably circulating through their veins, Caridad had a somewhat pronounced ass that men were inclined to show their unappreciated appreciation for everywhere she went" (26). After Caridad's high school sweetheart impregnates then dumps her, Caridad "no longer discriminated between giving her love to Memo and only to Memo whenever he wanted it and loving anyone she met at the bars who vaguely resembled Memo" (27). One night on her way home to her mother's house she is raped, slashed, and mutilated by a malogra, a sort of physical manifestation of evil thoughts, in this case the hatred and misogyny directed by Anglo, Mexican, and Chicano cultures towards a woman who transgresses sexual boundaries.

La Loca prays for her sister's healing, and Caridad experiences a miraculous recovery in which all her scars disappear overnight. Changed by this experience, Caridad ceases to give her body sexually and becomes a curandera, studying with the old woman from Mexico, Doña Felicia. Caridad retreats to the mountains of northern New Mexico, living in a cave like the mystics of old until she is discovered by a devoutly religious Catholic called Francisco el Penitente and several of his order's brothers. Although she has gone to the cave in order to meditate on her sexual attraction to a mysterious, dark-skinned woman and simply wants to be left alone, Francisco el Penitente decides she must be a holy woman or saint, especially after she is magically able to resist being carried off by the four men. Word soon spreads about her, although not in the way Francisco hopes: "Not only the nuevo mejicano–style Spanish Catholics went to see her but also Natives from the pueblos, some who were Christian and some who were not. . . . The word had even gotten as far as Sonora to Yaqui land. The stories grew until some began to say that she was the ghost of Lozen, Warm Springs Apache mystic woman warrior, sister of the great chief Victorio who had vowed 'to make war against the white man forever.' . . . Yes, perhaps this mountain woman was not the one the Penitente brothers thought her to be, but a spirit-memory, and that was why she was not overcome by them" (87–88). Like her semimythical sisters, Caridad is both human and more than human, an individual as well as an actor in a myth larger than any individual life. After her return from the mountain cave, Caridad discovers that the beautiful dark woman with whom she has fallen in love is half Pueblo and half Mexican. They journey together to Acoma Pueblo but are followed there by Francisco, who has become obsessed with Caridad and is stalking her in an attempt to bring her into the controlling sphere of Church doctrine. He is desperate to remove her and her healing powers from the religiously hybridized prayers and cures she practices and especially away from the impure female sexuality and polluted cultural mixing her dark Indian lover symbolizes. The two women flee from him, leaping hand in hand off the top of Acoma mesa. Like Esperanza, they do not really die, however, but are swallowed up by the sacred earth to live out eternity together in the spirit world upon which Acoma Pueblo rests.

Although she is already of mixed ancestry, Caridad allies herself even further with the Pueblo world through the body of her lover. Her alliance, however, violates all utopic visions of racial and cultural purity and of the Church's vision of tightly controlled female sexuality. The world of indigenous religion is presented here as more accepting than Anglo, Chicano, or Mexican worlds of both spiritual hybridity and varying sexual identities. Caridad's life and semi-death offers her mother yet another vision of how to build a utopia that rests upon rather than eradicates difference.

Fe (Faith), the third allegorical sister, is destroyed utterly by her journey into the forbidden realms of Anglo society but mainly by her abandonment of the possibility for utopic transformation inherent in Castillo's vision of the borderlands. As a sardonic reading of her name suggests, Fe is stubborn, blind, uncompromising, and demanding. She feels no pride in the Chicano culture of her family or community or the Mexican culture most closely represented, albeit in a romanticized form, by Doña Felicia. Fe takes pride instead in her pale complexion as a door into Anglo culture and out of the borderlands. She places all her faith in the vision of Anglo American utopia, working herself to death in a high-tech weapons factory that is poisoning its mostly Chicana work force with illegal chemicals. She ignores all signs of health problems, however, in her drive to acquire a house in the suburbs, a microwave, a VCR, and a new car. Like her sisters Esperanza and Caridad, Fe pays with her life, but unlike them, Fe dies completely; not even her ghost returns to the land of the living.

Ironically, however, it is Chicano culture that most brutally injures Fe. Her belief in what her life should be is structured not only by the Anglo dream of financial success but the equally strong Chicano ideal of marriage as the only proper road for a woman to follow. Fe imagines the day of her wedding to her Chicano fiancée, Tom, as the most important day of her life and one she has dreamed of since childhood. On the eve of the ceremony, after the dresses have been fitted for the bride and her four Anglo bridesmaids, Tom dumps her. Fe suffers a nervous breakdown, screaming nonstop for months and permanently injuring her vocal cords, while her sister La Loca prays for her, though "above all, she prayed for Tom, because like so many hispanos, neuvo mexicanos, whatever he wanted to call himself, something about giving himself over to a woman was worse than having lunch with the devil" (32).

It is only in her madness that Fe is able to vocalize her true feelings about what has happened to her. Once she regains her sanity and reenters the strict social boundaries of her world, her voice literally and symbolically disappears, and throughout the rest of the novel she can speak only in a hoarse whisper. Fe's identity, balanced precariously at the point where Anglo insistence on white, middle-class values converges with Chicano insistence on marriage for women, shatters when Tom's fear of women overcomes him. Still, caught within the bounds of patriarchal constraints slicing through

Anglo culture and the Chicano borderlands, none of the women involved are willing to blame Tom directly. Regarding her son's behavior, Tom's mother sheepishly tells Sofia, "You know how men are" (31), and Sofia, who recalls being deserted years earlier by her own husband after he had gambled away all their money and most of her land, merely nods her head in long-suffering acquiescence.

When Fe begins working at the weapons factory (after being informed her injured voice will prevent her from getting a promotion at the bank), she is marked by her Anglo supervisors as a "striver," unlike her fellow workers, nearly all of whom are Chicanas unwilling to kowtow or sell-out, as Sándoval terms it, to their condescending white bosses. Her reward for adopting the materialistic and aggressively ambitious attitudes of Anglo society is to be "chosen" from among the other women to work alone in the basement of the building with the most dangerous, and illegal, of the chemicals with which the factory is poisoning its workers. Despite the obvious and horrific effects on her health, Fe values her paycheck, her position of power over the other women, and most importantly, her faith in Anglo cultural superiority to such an extent she refuses to believe her Anglo bosses would endanger their workers. Like the character of Rocky in Silko's *Ceremony*, Fe is swallowed alive by her colonizer's culture or by the mythic version of utopia that culture presents. Fe, however, is colonized by more than one culture. Her faith is misplaced, or perhaps betrayed, by both/all sides of the multiple borders constructing her world and her identity. As a result, she dies a horrible death, eaten alive by cancers and, unlike Esperanza and Caridad, never returns from beyond the boundaries of her death.

By the end of the novel, as in the original myth, Sophia (Wisdom) has lost her daughters, but this Sophia does not stand helplessly weeping over their graves in testimony to the doomed nature of human society. Instead she learns a valuable lesson from the life and death of each of her daughters and vows not to lament the borders that have destroyed her children but to alter them and her own identity in the process. She is the first character to fully embrace the possibility of transformation and revision that is also part of the borderlands and, Castillo suggests, the only road to finally establishing a Chicana utopic vision. She does not attempt to escape the borderlands as Esperanza did, nor does she try to erase the marks of difference, like her brown skin or Spanish-inflected English that identify her as a borderlands inhabitant, as Fe did. Sofia attempts to transform the borderlands into a new space, shaped by Anglo, Mexican, and Chicano beliefs, but molded as well into a form that is entirely new, both like and unlike its predecessors.

Although men are not explicitly excluded (a gringo who raises peacocks on his small farm, for instance, is welcomed), this is a distinctly feminist utopia. Sofia's first step in the transformational process is to gather a squad of comadres and get herself acknowledged as mayor of Tome. Guided by the inspirations and warnings she draws from her daughters' lives and deaths, and in some cases their ghosts, she comes up with a plan to save the town, here the mythical heart of Chicano culture, a sort of feminist Aztlán, which is dying in the modern West. Like her daughters, the town is trapped between and within cultures, bound on all sides by borders that paradoxically must be crossed but which can destroy those who do so. The town's reaction to the changing shape of the modern West has been to dig in its heels and cling desperately to traditional Chicano rural culture, to resist rather than embrace change and the continuously evolving differences it represents. As a result, the town is being slowly crushed by the forces moving in the outside world. Nearly all the old families, both rich and poor, have lost their ancestral holdings, forced to sell to Anglo retirees and wealthy vacationers as taxes rise and subsistence farming and ranching become less and less feasible. Unable to find work, families are deserting the land and children are moving away to Albuquerque and Phoenix. Castillo writes, "The truth is that most people had not been able to live off their land for the better part of the last fifty years" (139).

Castillo blames this, in part, on "outsiders" who have overgrazed and overused the land so that much of it is unfit for raising crops or livestock. She repeats a common mythic trope found in Chicano literature about the region that holds that the old Hispanic inhabitants of the Southwest were, like the Native Americans they displaced, more in touch with nature than later Anglo arrivals and lived in sustainable harmony with the natural world. As Limerick shows, however, this myth has no basis in reality. Much of the Southwest, including New Mexico, was heavily overgrazed by early Spanish homesteaders, a practice that has been carried on by their descendants. And, as Castillo tends to gloss over in this work, all the land (overgrazed or otherwise) was stolen by the Spanish and their descendants from its original inhabitants, who certainly perceived the Spanish as brutal colonizers and "outsiders," whether their farming and grazing practices were sustainable or not. Castillo is inhabiting and invoking what Padilla terms "the geography of the past" (x). Padilla argues that for many writers, "their nostalgia for an earlier world produced not a non-critical reaction to loss, but an oppositional response to displacement, albeit a response often deeply mediated by a language of accommodation" (x). The accommodation in *So Far* often does veer into the noncritical, however, offering a romanticized, mythologized vision of a carefully cleansed history. Like its Anglo counterpart, this version of a mythic frontier past attempts to justify the actions and presence of colonizers by viewing them as having successfully created a rural utopia, while resolutely ignoring the fate of the peoples displaced in order to provide them with farms and ranches, however well managed. Castillo's vision is somewhat more complex than this. Modern Indians are portrayed as colonized and often exploited, but in an ironic mirroring of Limerick's identification of a popularly perceived discontinuity between the frontier past and the Western present, no connection is ever made between their current state and the actions of early Hispanic settlers.

Sofia's plan to save the town of Tome, however, is to reach back into this imagined past and transform it into something new, a postmodern borderlands utopia. Her contemporary creation depends on a highly mythologized view of the Hispanic past in the region. She creates "Los Ganados y Lana Cooperative" and this becomes Castillo's matrix. The comadres who form the membership, and the families to whom they belong, begin to graze their sheep communally, learn to weave the wool and market the handmade products they create, and reestablish in modernized form the edenic, sustainable lifestyle of the past they view as their birthright, callously snatched from them by greedy Anglo newcomers. The citizens of Tome have, in a sense, Indianized themselves, much as Ruben and his friends in el Movimiento do, although the irony with which Ruben's actions are presented is missing here. Through this process, Castillo's characters cast themselves in the role of the native inhabitant with the most rightful claim to the land by virtue of their imagined tradition of sustainable habitation of it. To do this, of course, the previous inhabitants and their claims to the land must be minimized or ignored. This is an awkward imperial dance that both glorifies Chicano culture's Indian roots and at the same time denies them, since open acknowledgment of Native Americans would necessarily require remembering that the land now being claimed by Chicanos was originally Indian.

Castillo imagines this new Eden as constructed of both the business savvy often attributed to Anglo society and the community-based nurturing she identifies as Chicano and female. Penzenstadler claims this figuration of separate attributes identified as typically belonging to one culture or another is common in Chicano myths, especially about the modern West and Southwest, although she claims that combining those disparate characteristics in a utopic form is rare. The borders between cultures, separating and defining them within this utopia, are not destroyed, but Castillo implies they can be made easier to cross, and the crossing can be made less dangerous.

The culture in between, the Chicano culture that spans those of Anglo America and Mexico is affirmed as a mestizo entity and remains both a reflection of the cultures from which it draws inspiration and determinedly different from them. This is especially evident in the co-op, which extends itself successfully across those cultures and exists in large part because of its crossed and hybridized nature.

Just as the co-op can be seen as an attempt to hybridize and reform capitalism, Sofia's founding of M.O.M.A.S. (Mothers of Martyrs and Saints) is a similar move directed at the Catholic Church. According to the novel, the organization soon becomes a powerful, international entity with its annual conference "taking the cake over the World Series and even the Olympics" (249). Headed by Sofia and governed by a board of "La Blessed Moms" (252), M.O.M.A.S. appears as a sort of ironic counterpart to the male-dominated Church, with the only male participants being the deceased (martyred or sainted) sons of the members, who make regular ectoplasmic appearances at each year's conference. Castillo slyly pokes fun at the Church's fear of women by having her narrator indignantly declare that, despite rumors to the contrary, M.O.M.A.S. would never stoop to the level of the Papacy by forcing members to sit on a special chair designed to prove they were not men in disguise, as it was rumored the Church did after a medieval Pope was discovered to be a woman. "After all," her narrator says, "just because there had been a time way back when, when some fregados all full of themselves went out of their way to prove that none among them had the potential of being a mother, did it mean that there had to come a time when someone would be made to prove that she did?" (251).

Castillo's mythic town of Tome, saved by Sofia/Wisdom's ability to combine the contradictory Anglo, Mexican, and Chicano traits embodied by her daughters, provides an interesting inversion of the Christian myth that inspired it and an unusual utopic vision for a Chicano work. While viewing the West as both a frontier/border region and a New Eden are common tropes in Anglo novels, Chicano literature about inhabiting a borderlands or crossing borders is typically anti-utopic. Unlike Anglos, Chicanos who confront frontiers, according to Penzenstadler, usually do so reluctantly, realizing that they "can be destroyed in known ways if they stay where they are, but they may be destroyed in unknown ways if they cross" (164). No matter what choice the characters make, she argues, they can never win and generally embody a "theme of strength in defeat" (164). Many Chicano novels, she asserts, "are antithetical to the American Dream; there is a question as to whether the trip across the border was even a fair trade of one type of misery for another" (165).

Most of the novels Penzenstadler analyzes, however, are written by male authors. The only work by a Chicana she discusses is Sandra Cisneros's *House on Mango Street,* which she acknowledges presents a more positive vision of Chicano culture and life in the barrio and that also allows the Chicana protagonist to cross successfully from the Chicano world into the Anglo one, ending with the narrator's vow to return to the barrio and, in an anticipation of Castillo's novel, to transform it (170).

While I would be unwilling to argue that this is a specifically gender-influenced phenomenon in Chicano literature, *So Far from God* is anything but anti-utopic, although its utopic vision is a startlingly new one. While Esperanza (Hope) and Fe (Faith) perish when they cross over into the Anglo world, and Caridad (Charity) is destroyed for her sexual transgressions of patriarchy, Sofia (Wisdom), La Mayor Sofi, arguably triumphs over both male domination and Anglo exploitation, successfully creating a new center by drawing together aspects from all sides of the borderlands that shape her identity. Castillo posits the possibility of a new type of mythic space, neither Mexican, Anglo, or entirely Chicano but a shifting, hybridized vision influenced by, yet different from, all three. It is not a space that has escaped colonialism but has begun a process of decolonization though an acceptance of hybridization rather than a search for purity.

This is an atypical utopia in other ways, as well. Although Sofia becomes La Mayor Sofi and the founder of M.O.M.A.S., she hardly lives a life of endless ease or utter bliss. All four of her daughters are dead (more or less), and she is divorced and has lost the last of her family's land and house. But as the parable that forms the inspiration for the novel suggests, she has now truly grown into the meaning of her name, though Castillo seems to suggest the journey will never be an easy one. This is an Eden born of tragedy, sadness, and loss, determinedly ignorant of the tragedy and loss its own founding forced upon those it displaced. It does not seek purity, containment, or homogenization. Its promises—of affordable childcare, small home businesses, and sustainable subsistence farming—hardly rise to the grandiose, rose-colored heights of more traditional Anglo utopias, but Castillo's vision does offer an imaginative revisioning of the traditional myths from which it is born and a radical restructuring of the nature and function of borders. It is not that boundaries cease to exist in Castillo's Chicana myth. They are more than real and yet infinitely permeable, like the walls of blood vessels that by their existence both define the form and content of the fluid that flows through them, yet exist solely to permit continuous transfer and exchange of that fluid. To destroy them as border means death (the destruction of the borderlands identity and culture) as surely as to breach that border with oxygen and nutrients (new ideas and new ways of seeing the world) means life. In Castillo's utopia, survival in and transformation of the borderlands requires both boundaries and their transgressions, and the ability to build an identity through and across cultures and religions, history and myths, without erasing necessary difference.

Conclusion

Myth, Roland Barthes asserts, is a type of speech chosen by history. It has "a double function: it points out and it notifies, it makes us understand something and it imposes it on us" (117). Myth transforms history into nature, he argues, by giving historical intention a natural justification, thus making contingency appear eternal (142).

In this book I have attempted to analyze the modern development of what I argue is the most important myth in the American lexicon by tracing its permutations in the works of three contemporary Western writers. My hope is to offer critical interpretations of these modern versions of the frontier myth by examining the ways in which it has been constructed and deconstructed, challenged and evoked in the process of transforming history into nature, especially through the genre of the Western. The novels I have chosen, from *Blood Meridian* to *So Far from God,* offer templates of what Barthes terms the metalanguage of myth, a language that speaks of itself and its birth in history. The complex self-reflexivity of these metalanguage stories illustrates one of the main goals of myth—to direct future actions by justifying the present through naturalization of the past. These stories represent the narration of the modern American nation and help illuminate the relationship between culture, history, and myth and the role of art in shaping all three.

In America, the myth of the frontier has often served as the buttress of the idea of empire and as its mask. Barthes claims that it does not matter if one is able to see through a myth—the impact of its impression remains, which is perhaps one reason the Western in the form of novel, movie, or television program, has never disappeared from the landscape of American culture, even when it openly identifies itself as myth. This is especially evident in McCarthy, who deliberately strips bare his myths and his mythic cowboy heroes, without ever diminishing their power to move us. He renders his mythic stories, as Barthes would explain it, both full and empty at once.

Silko's novels are perhaps less anti-mythic than McCarthy's but even more obviously postmodern in their deliberate unmasking of the imperial intent behind the frontier myth and in their subversion of the idea of racial and cultural purity that underlies it. Cultural stories, heroes and anti heroes, remembered and misremembered histories are fashioned in her work into something greater and lesser than Barthes's idea of nature as the product of myth. Multiple versions of history are naturalized in her texts, even those that appear to deliberately contradict each other. Thus the cultural miscegenation behind her myths at once creates them and destroys the foundations upon which they rest.

Similarly, Castillo struggles to create a mythic metalanguage that accommodates both conquered and conqueror, even, perhaps especially, when the subject has historically inhabited both categories. The clash between history and memory, and their function as a birthplace for mythic narratives, is transformed in the decolonial space of her novel. The language history chooses is, in the hands of Castillo, creolized and hybridized, contained by the stereotypical bounds of the search for utopia in the golden West and at the same time exuberantly spilling over into some other, newly imagined space.

All of these authors are engaging in what Barthes terms the double function of myth. They point out and notify; they make us understand while forcibly imposing that understanding upon us; they make us see our myths *as* myths, without lessening their mythic power. Here is the challenge and the importance of interrogating myth and its role in directing the daily life of the nation. I hope that other scholars will carry this inquiry further.

Notes

Introduction

1. Edward Said, *Culture and Imperialism,* p. xiii.
2. I alternate deliberately between the term "Native American," generally preferred by Anglo scholars, and "Indian," which is the word most often used by Indians, especially those of my father-in-law's generation, in referring to themselves.
3. Raymond Firth argues that we must take for granted that over the course of time myths have been altered and garbled from their original versions, and he goes so far as to hypothesize that myths exist solely for the purpose of "sociological validation of an existing structure, the projection of the present back into the past" (209). Th. P. Van Baaren concurs, arguing that "The occurrence of changes in a myth . . . does not mean that the myth in question is beginning to lose its function and will probably disappear in time; on the contrary, changes in myth occur as a rule to prevent loss of function . . . by changing it in such a way that it can be maintained. By changing it, a myth is adapted to a new situation, armed to withstand a new challenge" (218).
4. If we understand the function of myths to be, as Lauri Honko claims, a symbolic structuring of the world, a system of social markers defining a group's identity, or as Raymond Firth argues, a sociological validation of existing social structures, norms, and values, then the idea that myths do not exist in or are not generated by modern societies becomes invalid. As the structures, norms, values, and identity of a society change over time, so must its myths, regardless of a society's degree of "civilization." As William Bascom points out, whether or not a society recognizes its own myths as myths, or calls them religion (or science) instead, is irrelevant.
5. Theodore Roosevelt, *The Strenuous Life,* p. 7–8.
6. Richard Slotkin, *Regeneration through Violence,* p. 5.
7. Said, *Culture and Imperialism,* p. xxv.
8. For more discussion of the Boone myth, see chapter 4 of this study.
9. For a further discussion of the ways in which National Fantasy is produced through American literature, see Berlant's *The Anatomy of National Fantasy.*
10. See Garry Wills's "American Adam" in *The New York Review,* pp. 30–33.
11. Emma Pérez, *The Decolonial Imaginary.*
12. Women of course also fought in the first Gulf War and were captured as well, but none were so publicly or deliberately dramatized as Jessica Lynch.

Chapter 1. Foundation of Empire

1. I use the term "palimpsest" here as Daniel Cooper Alarcón has employed it in *The Aztec Palimpsest:* "a site where texts have been superimposed onto others in an attempt to displace earlier or competing histories. Significantly, such displacement is never total; the suppressed material often remains legible, however faintly, challenging the dominant text with an alternate version of events" (xiv).
2. In *The Legacy of Conquest,* Limerick argues that the association of the Western landscape with "a potent and persistent variety of nationalistic myth" (30) coupled with the government's official declaration of the end of the frontier in 1891 resulted in a public perception of "a great discontinuity between the frontier past and the Western present" (31). The perception has persisted, she claims, in part because of the romanticization of the frontier experience and in part because such a discontinuity allows the grim realities of conquest and colonization to be viewed from a safe remove, as associated with the distant past and unrelated to the present day.
3. Slotkin argues, for example, that the common and extremely popular folktale regarding Daniel Boone's first meeting with his future wife Rebecca Boone is a version of this myth. The story claims Boone was hunting deer by torchlight one night when he saw two eyes shining among the trees. He raised his rifle to shoot but at the last moment stayed his hand. What he had believed to be a deer was actually Rebecca, walking at night through the woods. This portion of the story, though widely repeated, may or may not be true. Neither Boone nor Rebecca denied it, though their children, feeling it to be primitive and pagan and thus reflecting badly on their father, who was already well on the way to achieving mythic status, did so vehemently. We do know that Boone married Rebecca soon after their first meeting. Within the bounds of the myth working at the level of popular culture, this act would have been the proper fulfillment of the rules of the sacred marriage, which culminated the hunt and which decreed that woman or deer, married or slain, the hunter must love and honor that which he hunts for its sacred nature in order to receive union, and communion, with it. For a further discussion of the Boone myth as the first truly American (i.e., combination of European and Indian) version of the sacred hunter story, see Slotkin's *Regeneration through Violence,* pp. 152–56.
4. Bell, p. 124.
5. The connection of the symbolic cannibalism of the Christian eucharist and the figure of Christ with both Old and New world versions of the sacred hunter myth in which the hunter himself must die in a symbolic mirroring of the hunter as stag and prey has been noted by many; see Slotkin's *Regeneration through Violence,* especially chapter 2, "Cannibals and Christians."

Chapter 2. "Pledged in Blood"

1. They are also actual historic figures murdered, as the Dueña accurately asserts, in what is widely seen as Huerta's hijacking of the Mexican Revolution with the knowledge and complicity of the U.S. government.
2. Tom Pilkington, for example, in "Fate and Free Will on the American Frontier," contrasts the United States to Mexico by calling the United States the "land of freedom" where "accountability and responsibility are the necessary complements of free will and volition" (321), while Diane Luce sees Mexico as "a troubled Eden" (157), and Vereen Bell terms it "a totalitarian hierarchy . . . an ancient culture . . . a primitive one" (926) whose history is one of "horror and pathos" (924), and Daniel Cooper Alarcón argues that McCarthy has simply reproduced typical Anglo visions of Mexico as "Infernal Paradise."
3. Daniel Cooper Alarcón suggests in *The Aztec Palimpsest* that John Grady is not defeated by Mexico but, rather, in a neocolonial extension of Manifest Destiny, triumphs by returning from the hell of the prison like a Campbell hero returning from the underworld. I would argue, however, that although John Grady survives, he enters Texas much reduced from the figure that rode boldly across the Rio Grande in the opening chapters, returning *sans* Blevins, Rawlins, money, and ranch, and with a broken heart to boot.
4. Vereen Bell argues that this process defines much of McCarthy's fiction, which he says "always seem(s) to verge upon, without ever moving wholly over into, allegory" (922).
5. Cooper Alarcón argues that the myth being repeated here by McCarthy is that of Mexico as "Infernal Paradise," "juxtaposing the paradise of the hacienda with the hell of the prison at Saltillo" (92). McCarthy certainly relies on the rhetoric of such images of Mexico, especially seeing Mexico as a site of spiritual testing for Anglo characters. Cooper Alarcón writes that the journey of John Grady and Rawlins "closely parallels Joseph Campbell's paradigm of the hero's quest" (88). This, I believe, reflects McCarthy's interest in the rhetorical power of myths—witness the hellish underworld of womb and tomb to which Lester Ballard descends in *Child of God.* I would argue, however, that McCarthy seriously subverts many of the defining characteristics Cooper Alarcón identifies as "racist moves typical of the adventure novel" (71) in Mexico. The issue of language is an important example. Cooper Alarcón writes that "classifying the Other as inferior through inferior speech" (71), with Anglo characters speaking perfect Spanish while Mexicans bumble through comically broken English, is one of the traits commonly found in the Infernal Paradise tradition. McCarthy inverts this in *Pretty Horses* by having John Grady and Rawlins speaking poor, grammatically incorrect Spanish, while Señor Rocha, Alejandra, and the Dueña Alfonsa speak nearly flawless English. In fact, the Dueña Alfonsa speaks English more correctly than the two Americans. This illuminates an issue McCarthy focuses on in many of his works—social class. As much as race or nationality, the differences between the two Americans and the Rocha family revolve around class and secondarily

money, the same things that serve to highlight the differences between the Americans themselves.

Chapter 3. "The Acts of Their Own Hands"

1. In *Gunfighter Nation*, Slotkin argues that the idea of the "savage war" is both "a mythic trope and an operative category of military doctrine" (12). It operates on the assumption that no peace between the conflicting sides is possible, that therefore the only outcome is the total annihilation of one side or the other, and that the "other" side in American history has been most typically Native Americans, and later Mexicans, whose "savage" natures demanded a brutal white response. Slotkin proposes as well that "the Indian war also provides a symbolic surrogate for a range of domestic social and political conflicts" (13) by projecting class resentment outward against a symbolic, dark-skinned enemy who then becomes "the only obstacle to the creation of a perfect republic" (13).
2. This figure is discussed by Henry Nash Smith in *Virgin Land* in the chapter, "The Mountain Man," in which he traces the evolution of the-man-who-knows-Indians from Leatherstocking, who argued that each race, Indian and white, had its own gifts and should be treated with respect, to later trappers, mountainmen, and Indian fighters who "delight in scalping Indians" (83). Smith suggests this demonstrates that as the Western hero moves beyond the Mississippi, "he is becoming more and more fully assimilated to the mores of the Indian" (83). I would argue, however, that the blame for Anglo delight in scalping, as McCarthy so brutally illustrates in *Blood Meridian,* can hardly be laid at the feet of native peoples. It is more likely a result of the growing knowledge in the nineteenth century that the continent was not limitless after all, that whites would not be able to simply move Indians eternally westward. Once Anglos crossed the Mississippi and began to covet land formerly believed uninhabitable by "civilized people" and set aside, therefore, as Indian territory, the savage war became ever more brutal as whites struggled to justify, rationalize, and accommodate themselves to the idea that they would have to eliminate, and not simply relocate, Indians.

   It is true, however, that from the time of first contact, Anglos were adopting Indian foods, clothing, hunting and fighting styles, and farming techniques. Richard Slotkin, in *Regeneration through Violence,* argues that the figure of the-man-who-knows-Indians solves the problem of whites seeming to act more brutally in the savage war than the Indians they accuse, by seeing that figure as the result of a sort of social Darwinism, with superior whites drawing from the best of the Indian world and replacing Indians as rulers of the wilderness with Daniel Boone/Davy Crocket–style white men in the guise of "Kings of the Wild Frontier." See Slotkin's discussion in chapters 4 and 5 of *Regeneration.*
3. For a more in-depth discussion of these devices in the Western, see the chapters "Western Hero" and "Dime Novel Heroine" in Henry Nash Smith's *Virgin Land.*
4. Such openly environmentalist sentiments are not really unexpected in McCarthy. As Tom Pilkington notes in "Fate and Free Will on the American Frontier:

Cormac McCarthy's Western Fiction," McCarthy's only close friend within a literary community he makes a point of studiously avoiding was the late Edward Abbey, whom Pilkington describes as "a polemicist and passionate environmentalist" (313). "There are few technical parallels between their work," he continues, "but philosophically these two writers are very close" (313).

5. Kolodny argues in *The Lay of the Land* that the early Western hero's rejection of sexual union with a woman demonstrates a rejection of the incest inherent in sexual union with the female earth experienced as fruitful mother, thus explaining one impulse behind Leatherstocking's determined celibacy. Sexual union becomes possible, she writes, only when the female earth is experienced as tempting virgin rather than mother, implying "the seductive invitation to sexual assertion" (67) and resulting in an environmentally ravaged land, as viciously tamed and controlled as its human female counterparts.
6. In an odd echo of Kolodny's discussion of the American pastoral and the experience of land-as-mother and therefore sexually forbidden (see her analysis of Leatherstocking's celibacy), Boyd is never presented as the Mexican girl's lover but as her brother. When Billy asks the girl if she is aware Boyd had a twin sister who died at age five, "She said that she did not know that Boyd had once had a twin sister or that she died but that it was not important for now he had another" (323). Even the arriero from the opera caravan refers to Boyd as the girl's brother (327) though later corridos sometimes call him her nóvio.

Chapter 4. Decolonizing Imperialism

1. In *Finding Tongues in Trees,* Michael J. McDowell examines Silko as a Native American nature writer, explaining how her vision of landscape turns it into a character within the novel. Similarly Lee Schweninger, in "Writing Nature: Silko and Native Americans as Nature Writers," also discusses the characteristics of Native American nature writing as opposed to that of Anglos, though neither Schweninger nor McDowell specifically engage Silko as a Western nature writer, nor examine how her work is similar to or different from the writings of other Western authors.
2. Silko discusses the writers who have influenced her life and her work in an interview with Kim Barnes initially published in *The Journal of Ethnic Studies,* vol. 13 (winter, 1986): 83–105. It also appears in *Yellow Woman: Leslie Marmon Silko,* edited by Melody Graulich, in the chapter "Background to the Story."
3. In *Culture and Imperialism,* Said discusses this process in James Joyce's *Ulysses,* arguing the decolonizing native writer reexperiences the quest-voyage motif from which he had been banished by means of the same trope carried over from the imperial culture into the new culture.
4. Slotkin examines the captivity, redemption, possession, and exorcism of Mercy Short and the psychosocial uses to which her experiences were put by Cotton Mather, especially her role as an accuser of witches. For a further discussion of the Puritan origins of Anglo captivity myths, see chapter 5, "A Palisade of Language:

Captivity Mythology and the Social Crisis (1688–1693)," in Slotkin's *Regeneration through Violence.*

5. It is interesting to note that Silko is also of mixed blood, part Laguna, part Mexican, and part white. In an essay published in *Yellow Woman and a Beauty of the Spirit,* she recalls her shame and confusion at being asked to step away from the other, darker-skinned students at her reservation grade school whenever white tourists wanted to take photos of "real" Indian children.
6. Even Laguna Pueblo itself is the result of the mixing of numerous Keres (Pueblo) cultures, including clans from Zia, Hopi, Zuni, Cochiti, Jemez, and Domingo Pueblos in its founding at what is now called Laguna in the early 1500s. Silko's own ancestors, especially Robert Marmon, an Anglo who married a Laguna woman and served as governor of the Pueblo in the late 1800s, contributed to the "Americanization" of the Pueblo and later, in the 1920s, its remarkable revival of traditional dances and rituals. For more on this history, see A. LaVonne Brown Ruoff's article "Ritual and Renewal: Keres Traditions in the Short Fiction of Leslie Silko."

Chapter 5. Sanctioned Narratives and the (Non)Innocent Triumph of the Savage War

1. See Pérez's *The Decolonial Imaginary.*
2. Her idea is presumably taken from actual Mayan almanacs or codices, the four surviving copies of which are currently housed in museums in Dresden, Paris, and Madrid. Two of the most famous are the *Popol Vuh* and the *Books of the Chilam Balam.* Like Silko's fictional almanac, these works were transcribed by Indians who learned alphabetic phonetic Mayan and classical Spanish.
3. This story is from a 1991 interview conducted by David K. Dunaway. For further excerpts from this interview see chapter 10, "Simon Ortiz," in David K. Dunaway and Sara L. Spurgeon, *Writing the Southwest.*
4. Even in those instances where the destruction and disappearance of native cultures is presented as tragic, the "noble savage" rather than "savage savage" variation, it is nonetheless imagined as inevitable, the fall of a quaint but inferior people before the irresistible force of superior Anglo culture.
5. As many have noted, as far back as Henry Nash Smith's 1950 *Virgin Land,* this mythic trope was pervasive in the national psyche. It was quickly adapted to all aspects of American life and literature, even those far from the "frontier." The rescue of the captive white woman from the savage, usually dark-skinned Other who must be killed is a mainstay not only of Westerns but of everything from early detective stories to modern police dramas, reenacting the savage war and moving it smoothly to urban settings. This myth is especially effective during war time, with the captive white woman appearing in the hands of savage blacks during the Civil War and Reconstruction, in the hands of savage Huns during World War I, and savage Japanese in World War II. In the last three decades, Hollywood has turned the rhetoric of the savage war, complete with captive white women, on urban blacks, Arab terrorists, and Columbian drug lords, perhaps in response to a

vague, modern American discomfort with seeing Native Americans in that role. Since the 1960s, Westerns, in response, have come to either avoid Indian questions all together, focusing instead on white heroes battling savage outlaws, or presenting Indians in more sympathetic ways, as in *A Man Called Horse, Little Big Man,* and *Dances with Wolves.* This apparently redemptive move, however, still works to erase Indian cultures (and the threat they pose in revealing the hollowness of the savage war and other frontier myths) by presenting them as helpless, doomed, and vanishing.

6. Bergland discusses the image of Native American ghosts in the works of Washington Irving, James Fenimore Cooper, Nathaniel Hawthorne, Lydia Maria Child, and William Apess. Nineteenth-century anxieties about racial miscegenation and "the woman question," she says, were often projected onto the figures of Indians. Ghosting nonwhites and women, then, both silenced and controlled them, leaving them disembodied and insubstantial, and, under the gaze of nineteenth-century rationalism, merely a figment of the white male mind.

Chapter 6. Necessary Difference

1. The term Chicano/a is often, though not exclusively, used by Castillo. However, some explanation and background concerning the use of such identifiers is necessary. Many Nuevo Mexicanos, especially of older generations, prefer to call themselves Spanish or Spanish Americans, saying that unlike Mexicans or Mexican Americans, their ancestors did not intermarry with indigenous peoples, although this claim is widely disputed. Others, especially in the mid-West and West, prefer the more generic term Hispanic, while Latino/a is common on the East Coast and is often said to refer to those of Puerto Rican, Cuban, or Central or South American descent. Many politically active individuals, however, insist on Chicano/a, claiming the tradition of resistance, racial hybridity, class, and cultural pride associated with that term, although it is more often used by those of Mexican or Mexican American descent than by those of Caribbean, Central American, or South American descent.
2. For a further discussion of the perceived pollution and power of border crossers, see Henry Nash Smith's analysis of the Indian-like Indian fighters in *Virgin Land;* Richard Slotkin's reading of the traditional frontier hero, "the-man-who-knows-Indians," in *Regeneration through Violence;* and the examination of the character of Billy in chapter 3 of this text.
3. See, for example, Richard Slotkin's discussion of Puritan visions of a New World paradise emptied of Indians in *Regeneration through Violence,* and further notes in chapter 4 of this text on captivity narratives and Leslie Marmon Silko's *Ceremony.*
4. See Elsa Saeta's interview with Castillo in "A *MELUS* Interview: Ana Castillo," pp. 133–49.
5. See ibid., p. 147.

Works Cited

Anzaldúa, Gloria. *Borderlands/La Frontera: The New Mestiza.* San Franciso: Spinsters/ Aunt Lute, 1987.

Barnes, Kim. "Interview with Leslie Marmon Silko." *The Journal of Ethnic Studies,* vol. 13 (winter, 1986): 83–105. Reprinted in *Yellow Woman: Leslie Marmon Silko,* edited by Melody Graulich. New Brunswick: Rutgers University Press, 1993.

Barthes, Roland. *Mythologies.* New York: Farrar, Straus & Giroux, 1990. Translated from the French *Mythologies,* Paris: Editions du Seuil, 1957.

Bascom, William. "The Forms of Folklore: Prose Narratives." In *Sacred Narrative: Readings in the Theory of Myth,* edited by Alan Dundes. Berkeley: University of California Press, 1984.

Bell, Vereen M. *The Achievement of Cormac McCarthy.* Baton Rouge: Louisiana State University Press, 1988.

———. "Between the Wish and the Thing, the World Lies Waiting." *Southern Review.* vol. 28 (autumn, 1992): 920–28.

Bergland, Renee. *The National Uncanny: Indian Ghosts and American Subjects.* Hanover, N.H.: University Press of New England, 2000.

Berlant, Lauren. *The Anatomy of National Fantasy: Hawthorne, Utopia, and Everyday Life.* Chicago: University of Chicago Press, 1991.

Blake, William. *William Blake: Selected Poetry and Prose.* Edited by Northrop Frye. New York: Modern Library, 1953.

Castillo, Ana. *Massacre of the Dreamers.* Albuquerque: University of New Mexico Press, 1994.

———. *So Far from God.* New York: Plume, 1994.

Castillo, Debra. "Borderliners: Federico Campbell and Ana Castillo." In *Reconfigured Spheres: Feminist Explorations of Literary Space,* edited by Margaret R. Higonnet and Joan Templeton. Amherst: University of Massachusetts Press, 1994.

Clifford, James. *The Predicament of Culture: Twentieth-Century Ethnography, Literature, and Art.* Cambridge: Harvard University Press, 1988.

Cooper Alarcón, Daniel. *The Aztec Palimpsest: Mexico in the Modern Imagination.* Tucson: University of Arizona Press, 1997.

Daugherty, Leo. "Gravers False and True: *Blood Meridian* as Gnostic Tragedy." *Southern Quarterly* 30, no. 4 (1992): 122–33.

Douglas, Mary. *Purity and Danger: An Analysis of the Concepts of Pollution and Taboo.* London and New York: Routledge, 1996.

Dunaway, David King, and Sara L. Spurgeon. *Writing the Southwest.* New York: Plume Dutton/Signet, 1995.

Dundes, Alan. "Introduction." In *Sacred Narrative: Readings in the Theory of Myth,* edited by Alan Dundes. Berkeley: University of California Press, 1984.

Firth, Raymond. "The Plasticity of Myth: Cases From Tikopia." In *Sacred Narrative: Readings in the Theory of Myth,* edited by Alan Dundes. Berkeley: University of California Press, 1984.

Gunn Allen, Paula. *The Sacred Hoop: Recovering the Feminine in American Indian Tradition.* Boston: Beacon Press, 1986.

Hall, Stuart. "Cultural Identity and Cinematic Representation." *Third Scenario: Theory and the Politics of Location.* Rpt. from *Framework 36.* London: Turnaround Press, 1989.

Haraway, Donna J. *Simians, Cyborgs, and Women: The Reinvention of Nature.* New York: Routledge, 1991.

Honko, Lauri. "The Problem of Defining Myth." In *Sacred Narrative: Readings in the Theory of Myth,* edited by Alan Dundes. Berkeley: University of California Press, 1984.

Jagose, Annamarie. "Slash and Suture: Post/Colonialism in *Borderlands/La Frontera: The New Mestiza.*" In *Feminism and the Politics of Difference,* edited by Ineia Gunew and Anna Yeatman. San Francisco: Westview Press, 1993.

Kirk, G. S. "On Defining Myths." In *Sacred Narrative: Readings in the Theory of Myth,* edited by Alan Dundes. Berkeley: University of California Press, 1984.

Kolodny, Annette. *The Land before Her: Fantasy and Experience of the American Frontiers, 1630–1860.* Chapel Hill: University of North Carolina Press, 1984.

———. *The Lay of the Land: Metaphor as Experience and History in American Life and Letters.* Chapel Hill: University of North Carolina Press, 1975.

Limerick, Patricia Nelson. *The Legacy of Conquest: The Unbroken Past of the American West.* New York: Norton, 1987.

Luce, Diane. "'When You Wake': John Grady Cole's Heroism in *All The Pretty Horses.*" In *Sacred Violence: A Reader's Companion to Cormac McCarthy,* edited by Wade Hall and Rick Wallach. El Paso: Texas Western Press, University of Texas at El Paso, 1995.

Manley, Kathleen. "Leslie Marmon Silko's Use of Color in *Ceremony.*" *Southern Folklore* (1989): 133–46.

McCarthy, Cormac. *All the Pretty Horses.* New York: Vintage International, 1993.

———. *Blood Meridian, or, The Evening Redness in the West.* New York: Random House, 1985. First Vintage International Edition, 1992.

———. *Cities of the Plain.* New York: Alfred A. Knopf, 1998.

McDowell, Michael J. *Finding Tongues in Trees: Dialogical and Ecological Landscapes in Henry David Thoreau, Robinson Jeffers, and Leslie Marmon Silko.* Ph.D. diss., University of Oregon, 1992. Ann Arbor: UMI, 1993. DA9313306.

McWilliams, Sara E. *Disturbances: Figures of Hybridity and the Politics of Representation.* Ph.D. diss., University of Washington, 1992. Ann Arbor: UMI, 1992. 9230407.

Nash Smith, Henry. *Virgin Land: The American West as Symbol and Myth.* Cambridge: Harvard University Press, 1950.

Nelson, Robert M. "Place and Vision: The Function of Landscape in *Ceremony.*" *Journal of the Southwest* (fall, 1987): 281–316.

Penzenstadler, Joan. "La Frontera, Aztlán, el barrio: Frontiers in Chicano Literature." In *The Frontier Experience and the American Dream: Essays on American Literature,* edited by David Mogen, Mark Busby, and Paul Bryant. College Station: Texas A&M University Press, 1989.

Pérez, Emma. *The Decolonial Imaginary: Writing Chicanas into History.* Bloomington: Indiana University Press. 1999.

Phillips, Dana. "History and the Ugly Facts of Cormac McCarthy's *Blood Meridian.*" *American Literature* 68, no. 2 (1996): 433–60.

Pilkington, Tom. "Fate and Free Will on the American Frontier: Cormac McCarthy's Western Fiction." *Western American Literature* 27, no. 4 (1993): 311–22.

Quintana, Alvina. "Politics, Representation and the Emergence of a Chicana Aesthetics." *Cultural Studies* 4, no. 3 (1990): 257–63.

Roosevelt, Theodore. *The Strenuous Life: Essays and Addresses.* New York: Century Company, 1902.

Ruoff, A. LaVonne Brown. "Ritual and Renewal: Keres Traditions in the Short Fiction of Leslie Silko." In *American Women Short Story Writers: A Collection of Critical Essays,* edited by Julie Brown. New York: Garland Publishing, 1993.

Saeta, Elsa. "A *MELUS* Interview: Ana Castillo." *MELUS: The Journal of the Society for the Study of the Multi-Ethnic Literature of the United States* 22, no. 3 (1997): 133–49.

Said, Edward. *Culture and Imperialism.* New York: Vintage Books, 1994.

Sandoval, Chela. "Feminism and Racism: A Report on the 1981 National Women's Studies Conference." In *Haciendo Caras: Making Face, Making Soul,* edited by Gloria Anzaldúa. San Francisco: Aunt Lute Books, 1991.

Schopen, Bernard A. "'They Rode On': *Blood Meridian* and the Art of Narrative." *Western American Literature* 30, no. 2 (1995): 179–94.

Schweninger, Lee. "Writing Nature: Silko and Native Americans as Nature Writers," *MELUS* 18, no. 2 (1993): 47–60.

Shaviro, Steven. "'The Very Life of Darkness': A Reading of *Blood Meridian.*" *Southern Quarterly* 30, no. 4 (1992): 111–21.

Silko, Leslie Marmon. *Almanac of the Dead.* New York: Simon & Schuster, 1991. Reprint, New York: Penguin Books, 1992.

———. *Ceremony.* New York: Viking Penguin Inc., 1977.

Slotkin, Richard. *Gunfighter Nation: The Myth of the Frontier in Twentieth-Century America.* New York: Macmillan, 1992. Reprint, New York: Harper Collins, 1993.

———. Interview. *ABC World News Tonight,* May 14, 1999.

———. Interview. *Morning Edition,* National Public Radio, May 18, 1999.

———. *Regeneration through Violence: The Mythology of the American Frontier, 1600–1860.* Wesleyan University Press, 1973. Reprint, New York: Harper Collins, 1996.

Smith, Patricia Clark, and Paula Gunn Allen. "Earthly Relations, Carnal Knowledge: Southwestern American Indian Women Writers and Landscape." In *The Desert Is No Lady: Southwestern Landscapes in Women's Writing and Art,* edited by Vera Norwood and Janice Monk. New Haven: Yale University Press, 1987.

Spurgeon, Sara L., and David King Dunaway. *Writing the Southwest.* New York: Plume Dutton/Signet, 1995.

St. Clair, Janet. "Death of Love/Love of Death: Leslie Marmon Silko's *Almanac of the Dead*." *MELUS* 21, no. 2 (1996): 141–56.
Stoeltje, Beverly. "Making the Frontier Myth: Folklore Process in a Modern Nation." *Western Folklore* 46, no. 4 (1987): 235–53.
Tompkins, Jane. *West of Everything: The Inner Life of Westerns.* New York: Oxford University Press, 1992.
Trinh, Minh-ha. *Woman, Native, Other: Writing Postcoloniality and Feminism.* Bloomington and Indianapolis: Indiana University Press, 1989.
Van Baaren, Th.P. "The Flexibility of Myth." In *Sacred Narrative: Readings in the Theory of Myth,* edited by Alan Dundes. Berkeley: University of California Press, 1984.
Wallace, Karen L. "Liminality and Myth in Native American Fiction: *Ceremony* and *The Ancient Child*." *American Indian Culture and Research Journal* 20, no. 4 (1996): 91–119.
Wills, Garry. "American Adam." *The New York Review,* March 6, 1997: 30–33.

Index